CORE SKILLS

GRADE

8

Math

ISBN 0-7398-7037-8

2003 Edition, Harcourt Achieve Inc.
Copyright © by Harcourt, Inc.

Printed in the United States of America.

6 7 8 9 054 07

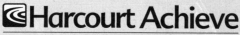

Harcourt Achieve

Rigby • Saxon • Steck-Vaughn

www.HarcourtAchieve.com
1.800.531.5015

Core Skills: Math
Grade 8
Table of Contents

Core Skills: Math, Grade 8, Table of Contents (cont.)

Core Skills: Math, Grade 8, Table of Contents (cont.)

Using Place Value

Write each number in words.

1. 20107 _____

2. 52037.2 _____

Name the place of the underlined digit.

3. 243,1_8_7.9 _____   **4.** 486.137_5_ _____

Write the standard form of each number.

5. 2.01 thousand _____   **6.** 8.7 million _____

Write in shortened form using the word *million*.

7. 35,842,000 _____   **8.** 60,000,000 _____

Compare. Use <, >, or = .

9. 88,205 ◯ 83,205   **10.** 64.5 ◯ 56.4   **11.** 241.307 ◯ 241.3070

Mixed Applications

12. The state of Texas had a population of 14.3 million. Write the population in standard form.

_____

13. Write a four-digit number with an 8 in the ones place and a 1 in the thousandths place.

_____

LOGICAL REASONING

14. A five-digit number contains the digits 1, 2, 3, 4, and 5. Use the

following clues to find the number. _____

Clue 1: The number is greater than 40,000.

Clue 2: The 1 is next to the 2.   Clue 3: The 2 is not next to the 4 or the 5.

Clue 4: The 3 is not next to the 4 or the 5.   Clue 5: The 1 is next to the 5 or the 3.

I

Rounded Numbers

Name the place to which each number appears to be rounded.

1. 320 _____

2. 182.4 _____

3. 14,000 _____

4. 16.11 _____

5. 36,500 _____

6. 8,000,000 _____

7. 6,800.9 _____

8. 2,700 _____

9. 8.014 _____

An exact number has been rounded to the given number. Name the greatest whole number and the least whole number that the exact number can be.

10. 230 _____

11. 4,200 _____

12. 56,000 _____

13. 8,000 _____

14. 650 _____

15. 7,450,000 _____

16. 3,800,000 _____

17. 2,370,000 _____

18. 120,000,000 _____

Round each number to the nearest hundred thousand. Then write the rounded number in shortened form using the word *million*.

19. 3,050,694 _____

20. 24,437,009 _____

21. 185,814,379 _____

22. 607,598,001 _____

23. 2,365,150,000 _____

24. 5,000,691,001 _____

Mixed Applications

25. If the smallest whole number that can be rounded to 500 is 450, what is the smallest whole number that can be rounded to 5,000,000?

_____

NUMBER SENSE

26. Use these facts to find the three-digit number. _____
- If the number is rounded to the nearest ten, the result is 20.
- If the number is rounded to the nearest whole number, the result is 16.
- The tens digit is the same as the ones digit.

Using Estimation

Choose the overestimate. Write **a** or **b**.

1. 74 + 85   **a.** 75 + 90   **b.** 70 + 80   _____

2. 38 × 32   **a.** 40 × 35   **b.** 35 × 30   _____

3. 672 − 235   **a.** 650 − 250   **b.** 700 − 200   _____

4. 43 × 9   **a.** 40 × 9   **b.** 45 × 10   _____

5. 58 ÷ 6   **a.** 60 ÷ 6   **b.** 50 ÷ 7   _____

6. 328 ÷ 27   **a.** 325 ÷ 30   **b.** 350 ÷ 25   _____

Give two estimates for each problem. Tell which is the closer estimate.

7. 963 − 857   _____   8. 39 × 48   _____

9. 4,630 + 2,397   _____   10. 782 ÷ 68   _____

Mixed Applications

11. Mr. Otto's car gets 26 miles to the gallon. He has 5 gallons of gas in the tank. He must decide whether to get gas now or continue to the next town, which is 130 miles away. Should he overestimate or underestimate the number of miles he can travel?

_____

12. Last month, Sally had expenses of $27.10, $53.50, and $19.82. Is $95.00 an overestimate or an underestimate of her total expenses for last month?

_____

WRITER'S CORNER

13. Write two word problems: one that is best solved by overestimating and another that is best solved by underestimating.

_____

_____

_____

Properties

Name the property shown.

1. $5 + 8 = 8 + 5$

_____

2. $4 \times (7 + 2) = (4 \times 7) + (4 \times 2)$

_____

3. $(3 \times 2) \times 6 = 3 \times (2 \times 6)$

_____

4. $25 = 25 + 0$

_____

5. $7 \times 9 = 9 \times 7$

_____

6. $1 \times 36 = 36$

_____

7. $5 \times (3 - 2) = (5 \times 3) - (5 \times 2)$

_____

Complete.

8. $139 + \boxed{} = 139$ **9.** $212 \times \boxed{} = 212$

10. $35 + (17 + 25) = 35 + (\boxed{} + 17) = (35 + 25) + 17 = \boxed{} + 17 = \boxed{}$

Mixed Applications

11. Amy bought 4 pens for $0.90 each and 4 folders for $0.15 each. Use the Distributive Property to determine how much she paid.

_____

_____

12. Show how to rewrite $21 + 47 + 9$ using the Associative and Commutative Properties so you can use mental math to find the sum.

_____

_____

MIXED REVIEW

Compare. Write $<$, $>$, or $=$.

1. $1.23 \bigcirc 12.3$ **2.** $3704 \bigcirc 3470$

Round to the nearest tenth.

3. 15.049 _____   **4.** 134.651 _____

Using Addition and Subtraction

Estimate the answer. Then find the exact answer.

1. Marla bought a new bicycle for $126.45. She paid $4.94 in sales tax. How much did Marla pay for the new bicycle in all?

   _____

2. Derek earned $10.00 baby-sitting for his neighbors. He spent $5.72 on a birthday present for his sister. How much money did he have left?

   _____

3. Individual times for the relay team in minutes were 1.05, 1.12, 1.07, and 1.02. Find the total time for the relay team.

   _____

4. The Amazon River is 6,411 kilometers long. The Mississippi River is 6,234 kilometers long. How much longer is the Amazon than the Mississippi?

   _____

5. A theater received $382.50, $411.75, and $243.00 from ticket sales on three evenings last weekend. How much did the theater receive in all for those evenings?

   _____

6. Tokyo is 11,532 miles from Rio de Janeiro and 6,053 miles from Paris. How much farther is Tokyo from Rio de Janeiro than it is from Paris?

   _____

Mixed Applications

7. Ian received an allowance of $30.00. He spent $4.77, $6.96, and $14.29 for cassette tapes. How much of his allowance remained?

   _____

8. Polly has saved $255.50 to buy a computer that costs $799.95. Her parents give her $145.00. How much more must Polly save before she can buy the computer?

   _____

EVERYDAY MATH CONNECTION

To record banking transactions in a checkbook, you add deposits and subtract checks. Find the final balance.

9. Balance: $780.42   Deposit: $66.50   Check: $347.95

   Final Balance: _____

10. Balance: $1,021.65   Deposit: $590.89   Check: $482.44

    Final Balance: _____

Problem Solving
Multistep Problems

Write the steps for solving the problem. Then solve.

1. The eighth-grade students are selling magazine subscriptions to raise money for a class trip. They earn $3 for every subscription they sell. So far, they have earned $228 of the $396 needed. How many more subscriptions must the students sell to meet their goal?

_____

_____

2. On their vacation, the Li family traveled from their home to a resort in the mountains. The odometer in their car read 35286.9 miles when they started and 35514.2 miles when they returned home. What was the distance from their home to the resort?

_____

_____

3. Geraldo bought a computer game on layaway. He paid $12 down and must make a payment of $5 each week for 4 weeks. How much will Geraldo pay in all?

_____

_____

4. Mrs. Bond made a deposit of $100 into her checking account. Then she wrote checks for $97.54 and $48.27. If her previous balance was $320.39, what is her new balance?

_____

_____

Mixed Applications	STRATEGIES	• Guess and Check • Write a Number Sentence • Work Backward • Use Estimation

Choose a strategy and solve.

5. Mikhail bought two copies of the same book and a tape priced at $11.95. He gave the cashier $60 and received $4.27 in change. How much did each book cost?

_____

6. Rhoda had $478.40 in her checking account. She wrote one check for $31.75 and another check for $85.50. Then she made a deposit of $150.00. What was her new balance?

_____

WRITER'S CORNER

7. Write a word problem that has more than one step in the solution.

_____

_____

Using Multiplication and Division

Solve each problem.

1. On each of 26 trips to a national park in June, a sightseeing bus carried a full load of 28 passengers. How many passengers did the bus carry in June?

_____

2. The driver of a sightseeing bus put 25 gallons of gasoline into the bus. The gasoline cost $1.31 per gallon. What was the total cost of the gasoline?

_____

3. An office paid $389.40 for 12 temporary workers for 1 day of work. Each worker was paid the same amount of money. How much did each worker receive?

_____

4. A police department bought 16 new cars. The department paid a total of $164,797.12 for the cars. What was the average cost of each car?

_____

5. Pam paid $8.75 per day to rent a VCR. She rented the recorder for 11 days. How much did she pay in all?

_____

6. Mary pays $0.95 per bag of ice for a party. Her bill for ice is $27.55. How many bags of ice does Mary buy?

_____

Mixed Applications

7. Mr. and Mrs. Rappold plan to stay at a certain hotel for five nights. They can pay $72.26 per night, single occupancy, plus $10.00 per night for each additional person. Or, they can pay $380.00 for 5 nights with no restrictions. Which option will cost the Rappolds less money?

_____

8. Brian bought some dog food for $0.57 per can and some cat food for $0.75 per can. He paid $5.85 for a total of 9 cans of pet food. How many cans of dog food did he buy?

_____

NUMBER SENSE

Find the missing numbers.

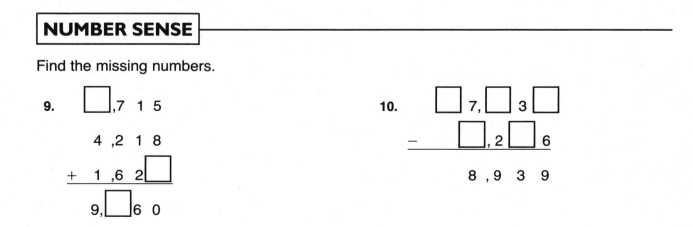

9.
```
   □,7 1 5
     4,2 1 8
 +   1,6 2□
   9,□6 0
```

10.
```
   □7,□3□
 −  □,2□6
    8,9 3 9
```

Dividing Decimals by Decimals

Find the quotient.

1. $0.2\overline{)3.8}$ 2. $0.5\overline{)7.5}$ 3. $5.2\overline{)1.872}$ 4. $0.008\overline{)0.472}$

5. $0.5\overline{)10.5}$ 6. $1.3\overline{)2.86}$ 7. $0.06\overline{)4.74}$ 8. $2.05\overline{)12.505}$

Find the quotient to the nearest tenth.

9. $0.4\overline{)2.544}$ 10. $0.06\overline{)1.4718}$ 11. $0.174\overline{)3.286}$ 12. $0.015\overline{)0.137}$

13. $0.8\overline{)1.925}$ 14. $0.03\overline{)0.611}$ 15. $1.06\overline{)4.012}$ 16. $0.029\overline{)4.666}$

Find the quotient to the nearest hundredth.

17. $0.8\overline{)4.388}$ 18. $0.24\overline{)1.64328}$ 19. $7.4\overline{)0.477}$ 20. $3.06\overline{)7}$

21. $1.7\overline{)0.923}$ 22. $0.85\overline{)9.916}$ 23. $1.02\overline{)26.14}$ 24. $0.3\overline{)6.515}$

Mixed Applications

25. The Bodacious Surfers Club bought 16 skimboards for $1,094.50. To the nearest cent, what was the average cost of each skimboard?

26. Lucy earned $146.84 for one week of work as a lifeguard. Meg earned $734.20 as a model for a television commercial. How many times greater were Meg's earnings than Lucy's earnings?

_____

_____

LOGICAL REASONING

27. Tom had $1.19 in coins. Vera asked him for change for a dollar, but he did not have the correct change. What coins could he have had?

_____

Interpreting Remainders

Solve each problem.

1. A sports car rally course is 80 miles long. The drivers pass through 6 checkpoints that are equally spaced throughout the course. How far apart are the checkpoints?

2. Hal's Charter Service will have 72 customers for a fishing trip. Each boat can carry 13 people. How many boats will Hal need for the trip?

3. Raffle tickets cost $1.50 each. Ruth has $8.00. How many raffle tickets can she buy?

4. Subway tokens cost $0.85 each. Rob has $5.35. How many subway tokens can he buy?

5. Neal bought 7 flashlights that use two size AA batteries each. Batteries are sold in packs of 4. How many packs of batteries should he buy?

6. Ms. Sims's car travels 24 miles on 1 gallon of gasoline. On a certain day, she drove 75 miles. How many gallons of gasoline did she use?

Mixed Applications

7. Joe drove 359.9 miles to Bayside. His car averages 30.5 miles per gallon of gasoline. How much gasoline did his car use?

8. Suppose you want to cut 2-yard pieces from 135 yards of fabric. How would you write the remainder to show how many yards of fabric are left over?

LOGICAL REASONING

9. An investor with $2,166 wanted to know how much money he would have left if he bought as many shares as possible of a stock for $8.50 a share. He divided by long division and found that the remainder was 700. Obviously, he could not have $700 left. How can you explain this?

9

Powers and Exponents

Write in exponent form.

1. $2 \times 2 \times 2$ _____ **2.** $5 \times 5 \times 5 \times 5$ _____ **3.** 6×6 _____

4. $4 \times 4 \times 4 \times 4$ _____ **5.** $7 \times 7 \times 7$ _____ **6.** 14×14 _____

7. $1 \times 1 \times 1 \times 1 \times 1$ _____ **8.** $10 \times 10 \times 10$ _____ **9.** $1.8 \times 1.8 \times 1.8 \times 1.8$ _____

Find the value. You may use your calculator.

10. $2^7 =$ _____ **11.** $9^3 =$ _____ **12.** $7^2 =$ _____ **13.** $8^0 =$ _____

14. $4^1 =$ _____ **15.** $2^4 =$ _____ **16.** $7^4 =$ _____ **17.** $13^1 =$ _____

18. $5^2 =$ _____ **19.** $10^0 =$ _____ **20.** $6^4 =$ _____ **21.** $5^4 =$ _____

22. $9^1 =$ _____ **23.** $7^1 =$ _____ **24.** $4^2 =$ _____ **25.** $2^3 =$ _____

Complete.

26. $2^{\square} = 16$ **27.** $6^{\square} = 1$ **28.** $\square^2 = 1$ **29.** $4^{\square} = 1$

30. $5^{\square} = 125$ **31.** $4^{\square} = 16$ **32.** $\square^4 = 6{,}561$ **33.** $\square^5 = 100{,}000$

34. $\square^2 = 25$ **35.** $3^{\square} = 27$ **36.** $27^{\square} = 27$ **37.** $\square^2 = 169$

Mixed Applications

38. The formula for the volume of a cube is $V = s^3$ where V is the volume and s is the length of each side. Find the volume of a cube when the length of each side is 3.2 cm. Write the answer in cubic centimeters.

_____

39. Jack saved 2 pennies today. If he doubles the number of pennies he saves each day, how many more days will it take until he has saved more than 1,000 pennies?

_____

MIXED REVIEW

1. Round 8.8095 to the nearest tenth.

_____

2. Write the standard form of 1.2 million.

_____

Order of Operations

Compute.

1. $5 \times (2 + 7)$ _____

2. $18 - (2 \times 6)$ _____

3. $(9 - 3) \times 7$ _____

4. $25 \div (10 - 5)$ _____

5. $4 \times 6 \div 3$ _____

6. $7 + 3 \times 9$ _____

7. $18 - 5 \times 3$ _____

8. $3 \times 7 + 12 \div 2$ _____

9. $36 \div 9 + 8$ _____

10. $8 + 8 \div 2 + 3$ _____

11. $12 \div 4 + 24 \div 8$ _____

12. $12 \times 3 - 4$ _____

13. $\dfrac{14 + 4}{3}$ _____

14. $\dfrac{8 + 4}{8 - 6}$ _____

15. $\dfrac{4 \times 8}{2}$ _____

16. $3 \times 4^2 + 8 - \dfrac{6}{2}$ _____

17. $3 + \dfrac{18}{9}$ _____

18. $6 \times 7 - \dfrac{18}{6}$ _____

19. $6 \times (43 - \dfrac{63}{9})$ _____

20. $9^2 \times (14 \div 2)$ _____

21. $\dfrac{4.2 + 3^2}{8.6 + 4.6}$ _____

Write the key sequence you can use to compute the value on a calculator that does not follow the rules for order of operations. Then compute.

22. $12 + 4 \times 3.2$ _____

23. $2.5 \times (20 - 5.5)$ _____

Mixed Applications

For Exercises 24–25, write the expression. Then compute.

24. Add the product of four and two to three squared. Then subtract one.

_____

25. Find the difference between the product of six and three and three squared.

_____

VISUAL THINKING ————————————————————————

26. Arrange the numbers 1–9 on the triangle so that the sums of the four numbers shown on each side of the triangle are equal. No number may be used more than once.

Language of Algebra

Write *expression*, *equation*, or *inequality* for each.

1. 24 + 38

2. $a + 15 = 40$

3. $17 - 9 \leq 10$

4. $8 + 47 = 55$

_____

_____

_____

_____

Write an example of each.

5. equation

6. algebraic expression

7. inequality

_____

_____

_____

Complete. Write $<$, $>$, or $=$.

8. $16 \times 5 \bigcirc 60$

9. $52 - 5 \bigcirc 47$

10. $4^3 \bigcirc 12$

11. $81 \div 3 \bigcirc 30$

Use the expression to write an equation.

12. 513 + 23

13. $15 \times 4 - 20$

14. $d + 18$

15. $\frac{a}{6} - 7$

_____

_____

_____

_____

Use the expression to write an inequality. Use $<$, $>$, $\leq$, or $\geq$.

16. 33 − 7

17. 16.5 + 8.5

18. $2x + 3$

19. $c - 10$

_____

_____

_____

_____

Mixed Applications

20. Write a numerical expression using multiplication that shows the number of inches in 3 feet.

_____

21. Write an equation using division that shows the number of dollars in 12 quarters.

_____

| **VISUAL THINKING** |

22. Write a numerical expression that shows the difference between the number of dots in each array. _____

12

Expressions
Addition and Subtraction

Write an algebraic expression for each word expression.

1. $12 more than the cost of a videocassette recorder, *c*

_____

2. the number of club members, *m,* increased by 5

_____

3. 16 less than the number of sandwiches, *s*

_____

4. the number of apples picked, *a,* minus 33

_____

Write two word expressions for the algebraic expression.

5. $t - 7$ _____

_____

6. $r + 1.2$ _____

_____

Evaluate the expression for $b = 4$, $n = 1.5$, and $x = 10$.

7. $n + 13$ _____

8. $b - 2$ _____

9. $25 - x$ _____

10. $8.5 - n$ _____

11. $b + 21$ _____

12. $6^2 - n$ _____

13. $b + n$ _____

14. $x - b$ _____

Mixed Applications

15. Jil paid $20 more for a car radio than she had expected. Write an expression that represents how much Jil paid. Let *p* represent the amount she had expected to pay.

_____

16. Pete bought a hardbound book on sale at $3.25 off the regular price, *r*. Write an expression that represents the sale price of the book.

_____

LOGICAL REASONING

17. If the value of $x - 10$ is 45, what is the value of $x - 15$? _____

Addition Equations

Tell whether the given value is the solution of the equation.
Write *yes* or *no*.

1. $4 + x = 27$, $x = 23$

2. $y + 11 = 33$, $y = 13$

3. $t + 10.4 = 17$, $t = 6.6$

_____

_____

_____

Solve the equation. Check your solution.

4. $s + 36 = 89$

5. $q + 19 = 45$

6. $29 + n = 55$

7. $47 + y = 99$

_____

_____

_____

_____

First, choose a variable and tell what it represents. Then, write
an equation for the word sentence.

8. Eight days more than the number of
days worked is 32 days.

_____

_____

9. The cost of a backpack increased by
$38.55 equals $198.17, the cost of a tent.

_____

_____

Mixed Applications

For Exercises 10–11, write an equation. Then solve.

10. Freya sold her coin collection for $95
more than she paid for it. She sold the
coin collection for $220. How much did
she pay for the coin collection?

_____

11. Abdul spent $3.39 more for a tune-up
on his car than he had planned. He
paid $48.87 for the tune-up. How much
had he planned to pay?

_____

WRITER'S CORNER

12. Write a word problem that can be solved using the equation
$x + 12 = 36$. Solve.

_____

_____

_____

14

Problem-Solving Strategy
Guess and Check

Solve.

1. Rachel paid $1.45 for postage with nickels and dimes. She gave the postal clerk 7 more dimes than nickels. How many dimes did she give the postal clerk?

2. Ralph mailed a total of 36 letters and postcards. He mailed 4 more letters than postcards. How many postcards did he mail?

3. Clive shipped 28 packages aboard a cargo plane. Twelve more packages were marked "FRAGILE" than not. How many packages were fragile?

4. Vanessa paid a library fine of $2.65 for overdue books. She paid the fine with 5 more quarters than dimes. How many dimes did she use to pay the fine?

5. In Exercise 2, suppose Ralph mailed a total of 40 letters and postcards. How many letters did he mail?

6. In Exercise 4, suppose Vanessa paid the fine with 2 more dimes than quarters. How many quarters did she use?

Mixed Applications > **STRATEGIES**   • Guess and Check • Work Backward • Write a Number Sentence • Find a Pattern

Choose a strategy and solve.

7. There are 32 students in a classroom. There are 3 times as many boys as girls. How many girls are in the classroom?

8. Chen bought a gallon of milk for $2.39, a loaf of bread for $0.99, and 3 cans of soup. He spent a total of $6.05. How much was each can of soup?

SCIENCE CONNECTION

9. Lila counted a total of 80 meteors in one hour during the Perseids meteor shower. She counted 44 more Perseids than sporadic meteors (meteors unrelated to the shower). How many Perseids did she see?

Subtraction Equations

Solve the equation. Check your solution.

1. $m - 6 = 32$

_____

2. $k - 53 = 24$

_____

3. $z - 40 = 35$

_____

4. $w - 17 = 67$

_____

5. $53 = g - 15$

_____

6. $t - 5.7 = 5.7$

_____

7. $1.2 = s - 4.9$

_____

8. $(9 + 12) = r - 8$

_____

First, choose a variable and tell what it represents. Then, write an equation for the word sentence.

9. Ten fewer than the number of band instruments is 47 instruments.

_____

_____

10. The number of meters decreased by 25.6 meters is 84.3 meters.

_____

_____

Mixed Applications

For Exercises 11–12, write an equation or equations. Then solve.

11. Fred paid $248 for a business suit. This was $55 less than the regular price of the suit. What was the regular price of the suit?

_____

12. Mike's age, decreased by the age of his 4-year-old sister, is 11. Mike's age, increased by his uncle's age, is 53. How old is Mike's uncle?

_____

MIXED REVIEW

Compute.

1. $2 + 7 \times 8$

_____

2. $4^2 + (21 - 15)$

_____

3. $7 + 13 \div 13 - 4$

_____

4. $(18 - 5) - 3 \times 4$

_____

Solve the equation.

5. $x + 8 = 29$

_____

6. $63 = 16 + c$

_____

7. $4.5 = y + 2.8$

_____

8. $z + 40 = 40$

_____

Expressions
Multiplication and Division

Write an algebraic expression for each word expression.

1. three times the area, a

_____

2. twice the length, l

_____

3. the quotient of the number of pounds, p, and 8

_____

4. the number of days, d, divided by 7

_____

5. the product of the number of miles, m, and 15

_____

6. the number of hours, h, divided by 24

_____

Write two word expressions for the algebraic expression.

7. $x \div 12$ _____

_____

Evaluate the expression for $a = 5$, $b = 2.4$, and $c = 6$.

8. $6a$ _____

9. $1.5c$ _____

10. $8b$ _____

11. $\frac{b}{12}$ _____

12. $\frac{a}{10}$ _____

13. ab _____

14. $\frac{b}{c}$ _____

15. $\frac{ac}{3}$ _____

Mixed Applications

16. Sara bought b bags of ice that cost $0.99 each. Write an expression that represents the total cost of the bags of ice.

_____

17. Paper towels are on sale at 6 rolls for n dollars. Write an expression that represents the cost of 4 rolls of paper towels.

_____

LOGICAL REASONING

18. If the value of $\frac{n}{4}$ is 4, what is the value of $\frac{n}{16}$? _____

Multiplication Equations

Solve the equation. Check your solution.

1. $7n = 56$

2. $2x = 94$

3. $6q = 312$

4. $2.7r = 8.1$

_____

5. $12t = 180$

6. $8s = 1,000$

7. $25p = 260$

8. $700 = 35b$

_____

9. $1.8k = 7.2$

10. $0.6m = 30$

11. $0.7j = 0.42$

12. $4.5y = 18$

_____

13. $5s = 615$

14. $0.4a = 9.44$

15. $51.6 = 2c$

16. $602 = 7k$

_____

17. $43e = 1,376$

18. $9.1h = 3.64$

19. $8n = 4^3$

20. $4t = (1.5 \times 8)$

_____

Mixed Applications

Solve. Write an equation for Exercise 21.

21. June owes a balance of $1,308.24 on a car loan. She has 9 more equal monthly payments to make. How much is each monthly payment?

_____

22. Roy works at Happy's Restaurant. He works 30 hours a week. Last week he earned $130, of which $40 was tips. How much is he paid per hour?

_____

SCIENCE CONNECTION

The formula $m = d \times v$, where m = mass, d = density, and v = volume, can be solved as an equation if the values for two of the variables are known.

23. Gold has a density of 19.28 gm/cm^3. Use the formula to find the volume, in cubic centimeters, of a cube of gold with a mass of 2.41 grams.

_____

Division Equations

Write the operation you would use to solve the equation.

1. $\frac{n}{7} = 20$

2. $4p = 6.4$

3. $x + 1.5 = 3.5$

4. $81 = y - 12$

_____   _____   _____   _____

Solve the equation. Check your solution.

5. $\frac{w}{3} = 8$

6. $\frac{n}{7} = 9$

7. $\frac{x}{10} = 17$

8. $\frac{b}{9} = 24$

_____   _____   _____   _____

9. $\frac{y}{0.8} = 2.9$

10. $4.2 = \frac{k}{6}$

11. $\frac{d}{4} = 37$

12. $4 = \frac{c}{17}$

_____   _____   _____   _____

13. $\frac{n}{0.47} = 22$

14. $4^3 = \frac{a}{4}$

15. $\frac{y}{1.4} = 35$

16. $24 = \frac{h}{31}$

_____   _____   _____   _____

Mixed Applications

Write an equation for Exercises 17–18 and solve.

17. When the total cost of a rental boat was divided equally among 5 people, each person paid $15.50. Find the total cost for the rental boat.

_____

18. It cost $120 to charter a large fishing boat. Each person paid $30 toward the cost. How many persons chartered the fishing boat?

_____

MIXED REVIEW

Solve the equation. Check your solution.

1. $x + 12 = 25$

2. $\frac{y}{4} = 18$

3. $b - 3.2 = 1.5$

4. $6x = 48$

_____   _____   _____   _____

5. $\frac{k}{1.2} = 6$

6. $2.2p = 121$

7. $l + 29 = 73$

8. $m - 91 = 4$

_____   _____   _____   _____

19

Exploring Two-Step Equations

Name the two operations you would use to solve the equation in the order you would use them.

1. $\frac{n}{3} + 6 = 9$

2. $4x - 5 = 20$

3. $\frac{a}{2.5} - 1 = 4$

4. $85 = 8y + 21$

_____

_____

_____

_____

Solve the equation. Check your solution.

5. $\frac{x}{5} + 4 = 9$

6. $\frac{d}{9} - 6 = 12$

7. $9w + 3 = 39$

8. $5c - 3 = 12$

_____

_____

_____

_____

9. $8b + 2 = 34$

10. $19 = 4a + 7$

11. $16 = \frac{t}{3} + 8$

12. $7k + 4 = 25$

_____

_____

_____

_____

Write an equation for the word sentence.

13. Seven less than the product of 11 and a number, c, is 70.

_____

14. Four more than the quotient of a number, *n*, and 8 is 28.

_____

Mixed Applications

Solve. Write an equation for Exercise 15.

15. The length of a swimming pool is 10 ft shorter than twice the width. The length is 35 ft. What is the width?

_____

16. Show the calculator key sequence you can use to solve the equation $\frac{x}{2.4} - 0.625 = 0.0625$.

_____

MATH CONNECTION

17. You can combine like terms to find the measures of the angles in a triangle. The sum of the measures of the angles of a triangle is 180°. Write and solve an equation to find the measures of the angles in the triangle at the right.

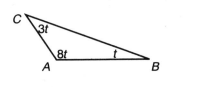

_____

20

Solving Inequalities

Solve. Write the whole numbers that make the inequality true.

1. $3a < 15$

_____

_____

2. $b + 12 \leq 19$

_____

_____

3. $c - 7 \geq 0$

_____

_____

4. $\frac{d}{4} > 1$

_____

_____

5. $4k \geq 36$

_____

_____

6. $x + 6 < 9$

_____

_____

7. $4n \neq 12$

_____

_____

8. $15 > 3y$

_____

_____

9. $p - 11 \geq 2$

_____

_____

Mixed Applications

Write an inequality for the problem. Then solve.

10. Hal wrote a check for $30. After writing the check, he had less than $450. How much did he have in the account before writing the check?

_____

_____

11. Six workers were paid less than $828 for a job. The money was shared equally among them. Could each have received $138? Explain.

_____

_____

LOGICAL REASONING

Assume that the given statement is true. Write *true, false, possible,* or *cannot tell* for each conclusion. Explain.

Statement: The Hoopsters won more than 12 basketball games.

12. Conclusion: The Hoopsters played only 12 basketball games.

_____

13. Conclusion: The Hoopsters won more games than they lost.

_____

Problem-Solving Strategy
Write an Equation

Write an equation for the problem. Then solve.

1. Eric has saved $587.46 to buy a used car. The car he wants costs $675. How much more money does he need?

2. A custom-made pair of shoes costs $225. This is 3 times the cost of a regular pair of shoes. What is the cost of a regular pair of shoes?

3. A truck can carry 7 tons of logs. Suppose that a truck is carrying a load of 4.7 tons. How much more could it haul?

4. A newspaper began publication in 1897 and was printed daily for 76 years. In what year did the newspaper stop publication?

5. Vera used 2.4 gallons of paint to paint her living room. This is 4 times the amount she used for her kitchen. How much paint was used for the kitchen?

6. The cost of a dinner is divided equally among 12 diners. Each diner pays $12.50 for his or her portion. What was the cost of the dinner?

Mixed Applications	STRATEGIES	• Write an Equation • Guess and Check • Find a Pattern • Use Estimation

Choose a strategy and solve.

7. Roy has a total of 10 quarters and dimes. The value of the coins is $2.05. He has more quarters than dimes. How many of each coin does he have?

8. Dot wants to buy meat for $7.57, milk for $2.69, cereal for $4.08, and juice for $2.99. She has $16.00. Does she have enough money for all the items?

9. Harvey bought a used car. He installed a $212 stereo system and 4 new tires valued at $285. His car is now worth $1,742. How much did he pay for the car?

10. Marsha sold 2 cameras in January, 4 in February, 7 in March, and 11 in April. If the number sold increases at the same rate, how many cameras will she sell in December?

Primes and Composites

Tell whether the number is *prime* or *composite*.

1. 3 _____   **2.** 5 _____   **3.** 86 _____

4. 89 _____   **5.** 93 _____   **6.** 51 _____

Write the prime factorization, using exponents.

7. 18 _____   **8.** 34 _____   **9.** 48 _____

10. 56 _____   **11.** 16 _____   **12.** 72 _____

13. 54 _____   **14.** 58 _____   **15.** 60 _____

16. 100 _____   **17.** 140 _____   **18.** 200 _____

Write the number represented by the prime factorization.

19. 2×3^2 _____   **20.** $3^2 \times 5 \times 7$ _____   **21.** $2^3 \times 5^2 \times 11$ _____

22. $3 \times 5 \times 7^2$ _____   **23.** $5^2 \times 7 \times 11$ _____   **24.** $2^2 \times 19$ _____

25. $2^3 \times 3^2$ _____   **26.** $3^3 \times 7 \times 11$ _____   **27.** $2^4 \times 5 \times 13$ _____

Mixed Applications

28. Max has 36 tiles to use for a rectangular design. How many choices for the shape of the design does he have?

_____

29. The sum of two consecutive prime numbers is 52. Their difference is 6. Find the prime numbers.

_____

NUMBER SENSE

30. Which whole numbers less than 50 have prime factorizations composed of a prime number squared?

_____

Using the GCF and the LCM

Solve.

1. Toby fertilizes the plants in a nursery every sixth day, and May prunes the plants every fourteenth day. They are both fertilizing and pruning plants today. How many days will pass before both will again fertilize and prune on the same day?

   _____

2. Ramona is cutting tags for trees from a 27-inch strip of paper and from a 30-inch strip of paper. Each tag will be the same length. Each strip of paper will be cut into equal lengths. What is the longest length she can cut for each tag?

   _____

3. Viola is arranging mixed bouquets of carnations and roses in vases. Into each vase she places an equal number of each type of flower. If there are 48 carnations and 60 roses, what is the largest number of vases Viola could use and still have the same combination of flowers in each vase?

   _____

4. Pam can wash a car in 8 minutes. It takes Rip 10 minutes to wash a car. They begin at the same time. How much time will they spend washing cars if they finish at the same time?

   _____

5. Mort has a certain number of Venus's-flytraps to sell at his booth at a school science fair. It is possible to arrange the total number of plants into groups of 9 or 12. What is the smallest possible number of Venus's-flytraps he can have in his booth?

   _____

6. A 126-inch board and a 168-inch board are being cut for steps at a nursery. All steps are to be the same length. Each board is to be cut into equal lengths. What is the longest length that can be cut for each step?

   _____

MIXED REVIEW

Solve the equation. Check your solution.

1. $u + 26 = 73$ 2. $a - 115 = 247$ 3. $4n = 104$ 4. $\frac{x}{8} = 56$

   _____   _____   _____   _____

Write the prime factorization, using exponents.

5. 24 _____   6. 32 _____   7. 58 _____

Problem Solving
Making Decisions

Gina LaRosa needs a new dress for the high school prom. Gina and her family are considering the following options.

Option A: Gina can buy a formal that costs $250.
Option B: Gina can rent a formal for $75.
Option C: Mrs. LaRosa can take 4 hours off from her work and make a dress. She earns $20 per hour, which she would lose by not working. She would need to buy 8 yards of material for the dress at $7.50 per yard, a pattern for $4.95, and other items for $9.45.

1. How much in earnings would Mrs. LaRosa lose by making the dress?

   _____

2. How much would Option C cost the LaRosa family?

   _____

3. Find the difference in cost between Option A and Option C, and between Option C and Option B.

   _____

4. Which option do you think the LaRosa family should choose? Give reasons for your answer.

   _____

   _____

Mixed Applications → **STRATEGIES** • Guess and Check • Draw a Diagram
• Write an Equation • Use Estimation

Choose a strategy and solve.

5. Mrs. Dunkelman works as a free-lance artist. She earns $20.25 per hour. Last week she worked 39 hours. About how much did she earn last week?

   _____

6. The price of a framed picture is $28 less than twice the price of an unframed picture. The price of a framed picture is $70. What is the price of an unframed picture?

   _____

Equivalent Fractions and Mixed Numbers

Write three equivalent fractions for each fraction.

1. $\frac{3}{8}$ _____

2. $\frac{2}{5}$ _____

3. $\frac{5}{12}$ _____

4. $\frac{11}{21}$ _____

Write the fraction in simplest form.

5. $\frac{8}{64}$ _____

6. $\frac{48}{96}$ _____

7. $\frac{11}{33}$ _____

8. $\frac{30}{60}$ _____

9. $\frac{18}{72}$ _____

Write as a whole number or a mixed number.

10. $\frac{45}{7}$ _____

11. $\frac{25}{3}$ _____

12. $\frac{19}{4}$ _____

13. $\frac{21}{5}$ _____

14. $\frac{33}{11}$ _____

Write as a fraction.

15. $2\frac{2}{3}$ _____

16. $3\frac{3}{7}$ _____

17. $6\frac{5}{6}$ _____

18. $3\frac{5}{8}$ _____

19. $6\frac{2}{5}$ _____

Mixed Applications

20. Caitlin has 8 rock albums, 2 country albums, and 6 jazz albums. Write the number of each category of album as a fraction of all her albums.

_____

_____

21. A mixed number contains the digits 0, 1, 2, and 4. The mixed number can be written as the fraction $\frac{81}{4}$. What is the mixed number?

_____

MATH CONNECTION

Fractions and mixed numbers can be shown on a number line.

22. Complete the number line by writing the missing fractions and mixed numbers.

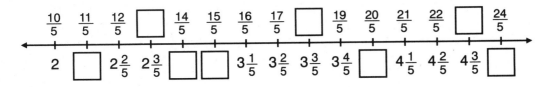

26

Comparing and Ordering

Write the LCD of the fractions.

1. $\frac{5}{4}, \frac{2}{3}$ _____

2. $\frac{1}{2}, \frac{3}{7}$ _____

3. $\frac{8}{15}, \frac{7}{20}$ _____

4. $\frac{1}{2}, \frac{1}{3}, \frac{1}{5}$ _____

Compare. Write $<$, $>$, or $=$.

5. $\frac{2}{5}$ $\bigcirc$ $\frac{1}{2}$

6. $\frac{3}{4}$ $\bigcirc$ $\frac{1}{6}$

7. $\frac{3}{10}$ $\bigcirc$ $\frac{4}{15}$

8. $\frac{2}{7}$ $\bigcirc$ $\frac{1}{2}$

9. $\frac{11}{5}$ $\bigcirc$ $\frac{9}{7}$

10. $\frac{12}{7}$ $\bigcirc$ $\frac{5}{4}$

11. $1\frac{4}{5}$ $\bigcirc$ $\frac{9}{5}$

12. $2\frac{3}{4}$ $\bigcirc$ $\frac{23}{8}$

Write in order from least to greatest.

13. $\frac{1}{2}, \frac{2}{3}, \frac{3}{8}$

14. $\frac{7}{10}, \frac{11}{25}, \frac{7}{9}$

15. $2\frac{1}{3}, 2\frac{1}{2}, 2\frac{5}{12}$

16. $\frac{7}{4}, \frac{4}{5}, 1\frac{9}{10}$

_____

_____

_____

_____

Mixed Applications

17. A survey of the time spent on homework showed that $\frac{1}{6}$ of an average class spent 90 minutes per day and $\frac{5}{18}$ spent 20 minutes per day. Which group of students was larger?

_____

18. List in order from least to greatest. $2\frac{3}{4}, 2.2, \frac{7}{3}, 2.4, 2\frac{7}{9}$

_____

MIXED REVIEW

Write the prime factorization, using exponents.

1. 16 _____

2. 24 _____

3. 56 _____

Write the fraction in simplest form.

4. $\frac{6}{9}$ _____

5. $\frac{12}{20}$ _____

6. $\frac{15}{45}$ _____

7. $\frac{21}{60}$ _____

8. $\frac{16}{12}$ _____

9. $\frac{8}{28}$ _____

10. $\frac{72}{99}$ _____

11. $\frac{56}{24}$ _____

Estimating Sums and Differences

Choose the best estimate. Circle the letter **a, b,** or **c.**

1. $\frac{5}{6} + \frac{6}{7}$ **a.** 2   **b.** 1   **c.** $\frac{1}{2}$

2. $\frac{11}{12} - \frac{4}{9}$ **a.** 2   **b.** 1   **c.** $\frac{1}{2}$

3. $4\frac{1}{10} + 5\frac{1}{8}$ **a.** 8   **b.** 9   **c.** 10

Estimate the sum or difference.

4. $\frac{9}{20} + \frac{8}{15}$ 5. $\frac{9}{10} - \frac{4}{7}$ 6. $12\frac{1}{5} + 7\frac{7}{10}$ 7. $8\frac{2}{3} - 1\frac{1}{6}$

_____   _____   _____   _____

Mixed Applications

8. One piece of jewelry contains $2\frac{1}{4}$ oz of turquoise. Another contains $2\frac{13}{16}$ oz of turquoise. About how much turquoise is in the two pieces of jewelry?

_____

9. Al got a difference of $\frac{13}{5}$ when he subtracted $\frac{2}{5}$ from $\frac{15}{10}$. Was his answer reasonable? Explain.

_____

_____

EVERYDAY MATH CONNECTION

The price of a share of stock in a company is listed on a stock exchange as a fraction or a mixed number. This number represents dollars or parts of a dollar. A "+" sign means the stock value has risen by that much from its value on the previous day. A "−" sign means its value has fallen by that much.

10. Estimate the total change in price of Jarvis Microchip Corporation stock over a five-day period.

	Mon	Tu	Wed	Th	Fr
Jarvis Microchip:	$36\frac{1}{2}$	$+\frac{1}{4}$	$+\frac{5}{8}$	$-\frac{1}{8}$	$+1\frac{7}{8}$

Estimate: _____

Adding Fractions and Mixed Numbers

Find the sum. Write the answer in simplest form.

1. $\frac{1}{5}$
    $+\frac{2}{5}$

2. $\frac{9}{15}$
    $+\frac{1}{15}$

3. $\frac{3}{8}$
    $+\frac{1}{2}$

4. $\frac{1}{6}$
    $+\frac{2}{3}$

5. $\frac{4}{9}$
    $+\frac{1}{4}$

6. 12
    $+\ 7\frac{5}{9}$

7. $3\frac{1}{5}$
    $+4\frac{3}{4}$

8. $3\frac{7}{9}$
    $+2\frac{1}{3}$

9. $8\frac{2}{5}$
    $+3\frac{1}{4}$

10. $2\frac{1}{5}$
    $+8\frac{2}{3}$

11. $2\frac{3}{4}$
    $+\ 1\frac{1}{5}$

12. 15
    $+\ 2\frac{5}{8}$

13. $\frac{4}{5}$
    $+\frac{1}{3}$

14. $\frac{2}{9}$
    $+\frac{1}{6}$

15. $8\frac{1}{2}$
    $+5\frac{3}{7}$

Mixed Applications

16. One day Mr. Ortiz drove for $6\frac{1}{3}$ hours. The next day, he drove for $9\frac{1}{2}$ hours. For how many hours did he drive during the two days?

17. A new swimming pool is being filled. On Monday $404\frac{3}{4}$ gallons of water were pumped into the pool. On Tuesday $358\frac{3}{5}$ gallons of water were added. How many gallons of water have been pumped into the pool?

MATH CONNECTION

A **unit fraction** is a fraction with 1 as the numerator. Some fractions can be written as the sum of two unit fractions.

Example $\frac{5}{8} = \frac{1}{8} + \frac{4}{8} = \frac{1}{8} + \frac{1}{2}$ ◄——— $\frac{1}{8}$ and $\frac{1}{2}$ are unit fractions.

18. Write five more fractions as the sum of two unit fractions.

Subtracting Fractions and Mixed Numbers

Find the difference. Write the answer in simplest form.

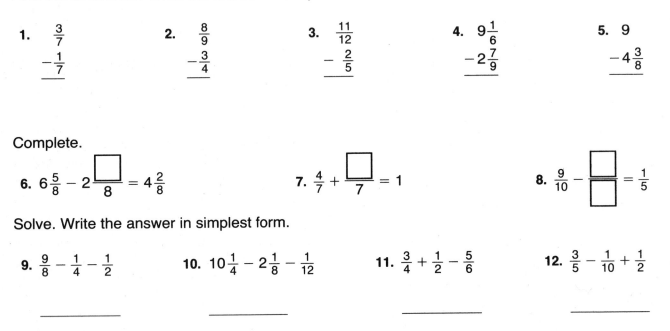

1. $\frac{3}{7}$
    $-\frac{1}{7}$

2. $\frac{8}{9}$
    $-\frac{3}{4}$

3. $\frac{11}{12}$
    $-\frac{2}{5}$

4. $9\frac{1}{6}$
    $-2\frac{7}{9}$

5. 9
    $-4\frac{3}{8}$

Complete.

6. $6\frac{5}{8} - 2\frac{\square}{8} = 4\frac{2}{8}$

7. $\frac{4}{7} + \frac{\square}{7} = 1$

8. $\frac{9}{10} - \frac{\square}{\square} = \frac{1}{5}$

Solve. Write the answer in simplest form.

9. $\frac{9}{8} - \frac{1}{4} - \frac{1}{2}$

10. $10\frac{1}{4} - 2\frac{1}{8} - \frac{1}{12}$

11. $\frac{3}{4} + \frac{1}{2} - \frac{5}{6}$

12. $\frac{3}{5} - \frac{1}{10} + \frac{1}{2}$

Mixed Applications

13. In 1963 the space flight of Valentina Tereshkova, the first woman in space, lasted $70\frac{5}{6}$ hr. In 1961 the space flight of Yuri Gagarin, the first man in space, lasted $1\frac{4}{5}$ hr. How much longer was Tereshkova's flight than Gagarin's?

14. In a recent year, among people 18 to 24 years old in the United States, $\frac{2}{5}$ had four years of high school and $\frac{7}{20}$ had some college or graduate study. What fraction of that age group had fewer than four years of high school?

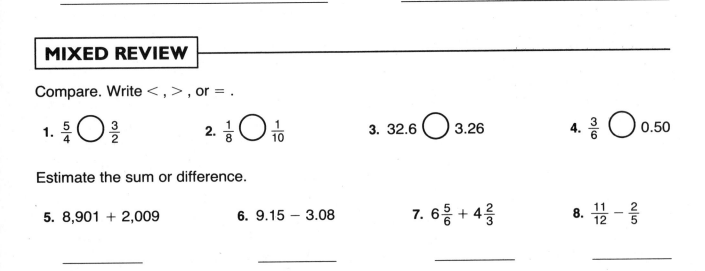

MIXED REVIEW

Compare. Write $<$, $>$, or $=$.

1. $\frac{5}{4} \bigcirc \frac{3}{2}$

2. $\frac{1}{8} \bigcirc \frac{1}{10}$

3. $32.6 \bigcirc 3.26$

4. $\frac{3}{6} \bigcirc 0.50$

Estimate the sum or difference.

5. $8,901 + 2,009$

6. $9.15 - 3.08$

7. $6\frac{5}{6} + 4\frac{2}{3}$

8. $\frac{11}{12} - \frac{2}{5}$

30

Problem Solving
Choose a Strategy

Mixed Applications	STRATEGIES	• Draw a Diagram • Guess and Check • Write an Equation • Use Estimation • Use a Formula

Choose a strategy and solve.

1. The Moros have a rectangular swimming pool in the center of their backyard. The backyard is $60\frac{1}{4}$ ft long and $32\frac{1}{2}$ ft wide. The pool is 25 ft long and $12\frac{3}{4}$ ft wide. How many feet does the yard extend beyond each side of the pool?

2. Lee needs 32 sections of fencing for the backyard. The fence will be in the shape of a rectangle. If 12 sections are needed for each long side, how many sections are in each width?

3. From her home Rhonda jogged 3 blocks north, 4 blocks east, 2 blocks north, 1 block east, 5 blocks south, and 3 blocks west. How many blocks from home was she?

4. Clint roped 53 cows this week. This is 9 more than the number of cows he roped last week. How many cows did he rope last week?

5. Rick works part-time at a bicycle shop. He worked for $3\frac{1}{5}$ hr on Monday, $2\frac{1}{2}$ hr on Tuesday, and $4\frac{3}{4}$ hr on Wednesday. For about how many hours did he work?

6. Jaime gave Fawn $0.95 in dimes and nickels. There were 5 more dimes than nickels. How many of each coin were there?

7. Abdul wants to hang a square poster that measures $1\frac{1}{2}$ feet on a side in the center of a 12-ft-long wall. How far from the end of the wall should Abdul place the side of the poster?

8. Binti saved $3 this week. Suppose she doubles the amount of her savings each week for the next 4 weeks. What total amount will she save during the 5 weeks?

Estimating Products

Estimate the product.

1. $\frac{3}{8} \times \frac{9}{10}$ _____

2. $\frac{4}{5} \times \frac{7}{9}$ _____

3. $1\frac{3}{7} \times 3\frac{7}{8}$ _____

4. $4\frac{1}{3} \times 3\frac{1}{10}$ _____

5. $5\frac{3}{5} \times 6\frac{3}{5}$ _____

6. $\frac{11}{12} \times 20$ _____

7. $3\frac{3}{4} \times 8$ _____

8. $\frac{7}{8} \times 10\frac{1}{7}$ _____

9. $3\frac{1}{6} \times 4 \times 5\frac{3}{4}$ _____

10. $1 \times 8\frac{1}{10} \times \frac{9}{16}$ _____

11. $12 \times \frac{11}{12} \times \frac{2}{5}$ _____

Estimate the product. Tell whether the estimate is an *overestimate*, an *underestimate*, or a *close estimate*.

12. $8\frac{1}{7} \times 7\frac{5}{6}$

_____

13. $5\frac{2}{9} \times 6\frac{1}{12}$

_____

14. $\frac{7}{8} \times \frac{3}{4}$

_____

15. $\frac{3}{8} \times 20\frac{1}{4}$

_____

16. $4\frac{4}{5} \times 9\frac{9}{10}$

_____

17. $7\frac{7}{12} \times 8\frac{1}{3}$

_____

Mixed Applications

18. A farmer planted crops in a $119\frac{7}{8}$-acre field. Corn covered $\frac{3}{8}$ of the field. About how many acres of corn did the farmer plant?

_____

19. Matt bought a used lawn mower for $\frac{2}{5}$ of the $280 regular price. After using the mower for one year, he sold it for $\frac{7}{15}$ of what he had paid for it. For about how much did he sell the mower?

_____

EVERYDAY MATH CONNECTION

Here is a recipe for whole wheat crackers.

20. Estimate the amount of each ingredient needed to make $\frac{1}{2}$ the recipe.

_____

_____

Whole Wheat Crackers

$1\frac{7}{8}$ cups whole wheat flour

$2\frac{1}{4}$ teaspoons salt

$\frac{3}{8}$ cup oil

$\frac{11}{12}$ tablespoon yeast

Multiplying Fractions

Choose the pairs of fractions that have a product of 1.

1. $\frac{1}{4}$ $\frac{2}{5}$ $\frac{5}{7}$ $\frac{5}{2}$ $\frac{7}{1}$ $\frac{5}{1}$ $\frac{4}{1}$ _____

2. $\frac{3}{8}$ $\frac{4}{5}$ $\frac{2}{3}$ $\frac{1}{9}$ $\frac{3}{2}$ $\frac{8}{1}$ $\frac{9}{1}$ _____

Find the product. Write the product in simplest form.

3. $\frac{5}{9} \times \frac{9}{5}$ _____

4. $\frac{7}{8} \times \frac{8}{9}$ _____

5. $\frac{5}{16} \times \frac{7}{15}$ _____

6. $\frac{8}{9} \times \frac{9}{8}$ _____

7. $5 \times \frac{9}{5}$ _____

8. $\frac{5}{8} \times \frac{5}{2}$ _____

9. $\frac{1}{4} \times 3$ _____

10. $\frac{7}{8} \times \frac{4}{5}$ _____

11. $\frac{1}{2} \times \frac{8}{9} \times \frac{3}{7}$ _____

12. $\frac{2}{3} \times 6 \times \frac{1}{4}$ _____

13. $\frac{11}{12} \times \frac{6}{25} \times \frac{5}{9}$ _____

Solve.

14. $\frac{1}{2} \times \left(\frac{1}{2} + \frac{1}{4} \right)$ _____

15. $\frac{3}{4} + \frac{1}{8} - \frac{2}{3}$ _____

16. $\frac{7}{10} + \frac{2}{5} \times \frac{1}{4}$ _____

Mixed Applications

17. Mona has 20 palm trees. Of these, $\frac{2}{5}$ are royal palms. How many of Mona's palm trees are royal palms?

18. Barney planted $\frac{3}{8}$ of his garden with tulips. Of these, $\frac{2}{9}$ were red tulips. What part of Barney's garden was not planted with red tulips?

_____ _____

MATH CONNECTION

Exponents can be used to indicate repeated multiplication of a fractional factor.

Find the product.

19. $\left(\frac{1}{5} \right)^2$ _____

20. $\left(\frac{2}{3} \right)^2$ _____

21. $\left(\frac{2}{5} \right)^3$ _____

22. $\left(\frac{1}{3} \right)^4$ _____

Multiplying Mixed Numbers

Find the product. Write the product in simplest form.

1. $10 \times 4\frac{1}{2}$ _____

2. $\frac{4}{9} \times 2\frac{1}{5}$ _____

3. $\frac{9}{11} \times 4$ _____

4. $2\frac{2}{3} \times 7$ _____

5. $7 \times 3\frac{5}{7}$ _____

6. $\frac{2}{3} \times 9\frac{1}{2}$ _____

7. $5\frac{1}{3} \times 6\frac{1}{2}$ _____

8. $4\frac{3}{5} \times 7\frac{3}{4}$ _____

9. $3\frac{2}{3} \times 9\frac{3}{8}$ _____

10. $\frac{1}{2} \times 2\frac{1}{4} \times 1\frac{1}{6}$ _____

11. $1\frac{1}{8} \times 2\frac{1}{4} \times \frac{12}{20}$ _____

Use a calculator to find the product for Exercises 12–14.

12. $\frac{5}{8} \times \frac{2}{5}$ _____

13. $\frac{1}{2} \times \frac{3}{4}$ _____

14. $1\frac{4}{5} \times 2\frac{3}{8}$ _____

15. The product of $2\frac{1}{4} \times 3\frac{1}{2}$ is $7\frac{7}{8}$. Find two other numbers that have a product of $7\frac{7}{8}$.

_____

Mixed Applications

16. April spread $12\frac{1}{2}$ lb of mulch. Ron spread $2\frac{1}{5}$ times as much. How much mulch did Ron spread?

_____

17. Yoko worked $1\frac{1}{4}$ times longer on the hydroponic garden project than Mark. Mark worked on the project for $4\frac{3}{8}$ hours. For how many hours did Yoko and Mark work on the project?

_____

MIXED REVIEW

Estimate the product.

1. 196×9 _____

2. 8.2×12.9 _____

3. $\frac{7}{8} \times \frac{5}{6}$ _____

4. $4\frac{1}{4} \times 9\frac{4}{5}$ _____

5. 2.5×0.48 _____

6. 15.8×1.9 _____

7. $1\frac{7}{9} \times \frac{8}{9}$ _____

8. $\frac{3}{4} \times 77$ _____

Estimating Quotients

Tell whether the quotient is *less than 1* or *greater than 1*.

1. $\frac{2}{3} \div \frac{1}{2}$ _____

2. $\frac{1}{4} \div \frac{2}{5}$ _____

3. $\frac{2}{5} \div \frac{4}{7}$ _____

4. $\frac{5}{6} \div \frac{1}{4}$ _____

5. $\frac{1}{3} \div \frac{1}{2}$ _____

6. $\frac{5}{8} \div \frac{3}{5}$ _____

7. $\frac{11}{12} \div \frac{5}{6}$ _____

8. $\frac{2}{3} \div \frac{3}{4}$ _____

9. $\frac{1}{6} \div \frac{1}{5}$ _____

10. $\frac{2}{9} \div \frac{1}{5}$ _____

11. $\frac{15}{16} \div \frac{1}{10}$ _____

12. $\frac{1}{2} \div \frac{6}{11}$ _____

Use compatible numbers to estimate the quotient.

13. $9\frac{1}{4} \div 2\frac{7}{8}$ _____

14. $13\frac{5}{6} \div 7\frac{1}{3}$ _____

15. $4\frac{4}{5} \div 9\frac{9}{10}$ _____

16. $6\frac{1}{3} \div 6\frac{1}{4}$ _____

17. $8\frac{3}{8} \div \frac{5}{4}$ _____

18. $1\frac{3}{4} \div 3\frac{1}{9}$ _____

19. $15\frac{11}{14} \div 3\frac{8}{9}$ _____

20. $5\frac{1}{5} \div 15\frac{3}{8}$ _____

21. $5\frac{7}{10} \div 30\frac{2}{9}$ _____

Mixed Applications

22. Julio fertilized 41 plants in $2\frac{1}{4}$ hours. About how many plants did Julio fertilize in 1 hour?

_____

23. Molly loads $64\frac{1}{3}$ lb of potatoes into $7\frac{3}{4}$ bags. About how many pounds of potatoes are in each bag?

_____

LOGICAL REASONING ————————————————————————

24. Tim had some $1 bills in his wallet on Monday. He spent half of the bills on Tuesday, half of what was left on Wednesday, and half of what was left on Thursday. What fraction of the original number of $1 bills did he spend on Thursday?

_____

Dividing Fractions

Find the quotient. Write the quotient in simplest form.

1. $\frac{2}{3} \div \frac{8}{15}$ _____

2. $8 \div \frac{4}{5}$ _____

3. $\frac{7}{12} \div \frac{9}{17}$ _____

4. $\frac{9}{10} \div 9$ _____

5. $\frac{23}{24} \div \frac{9}{15}$ _____

6. $\frac{7}{8} \div \frac{7}{15}$ _____

7. $\frac{1}{9} \div \frac{9}{10}$ _____

8. $\frac{2}{5} \div 18$ _____

9. $12 \div \frac{3}{4}$ _____

10. $\frac{1}{2} \div 24$ _____

11. $\frac{5}{7} \div \frac{13}{14}$ _____

12. $\frac{9}{20} \div \frac{5}{6}$ _____

Solve.

13. $\frac{5}{6} - \left(\frac{1}{2} \div \frac{3}{4} \right)$ _____

14. $\frac{5}{4} \div \frac{3}{4} - \frac{1}{5}$ _____

Mixed Applications

15. How many boards, each $\frac{3}{4}$ yd long, can be cut from a piece of wood that is 6 yards long? Will there be any wood left over?

_____

16. John can wash $\frac{1}{4}$ of a car in 1 minute. How many cars can he wash in 19 minutes?

_____

NUMBER SENSE

Use the numbers to write a fraction division problem with a quotient equal to the number in the box.

17. 8, 3, 4, 1 $\boxed{1\frac{1}{2}}$ _____

18. 4, 9, 24 $\boxed{54}$ _____

19. 4, 2, 7, 9 $\boxed{1\frac{5}{9}}$ _____

20. 2, 3, 6, 7 $\boxed{\frac{7}{9}}$ _____

21. 5, 10, 12 $\boxed{24}$ _____

22. 2, 7, 8, 13, $\boxed{2\frac{2}{13}}$ _____

Problem-Solving Strategy
Solve a Simpler Problem

1. The numbers 3, 6, and 10 can be represented by triangular arrays of dots. What is the next greater number that can be represented by a triangular array?

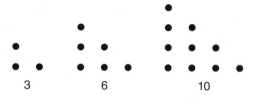

3   6   10

2. Some numbers can be represented by square arrays of dots. Four is the smallest number that can be represented by such an array. What is the greatest number less than 50 that can be represented by a square array of dots?

Mixed Applications → **STRATEGIES** • Solve a Simpler Problem • Draw a Diagram • Write an Equation • Use Estimation

Choose a strategy and solve.

3. At a meeting, every person shook hands with every other person exactly one time. There were a total of 28 handshakes. Find the number of people at the meeting.

4. Robert paid $207.95 for a lawn mower, $18.80 for a rake, $49.13 for an edger, and $12.65 for trash bags. About how much did he pay?

5. Nori paid $4 more than twice the amount of a pair of utility gloves for a shovel. She paid $16 for the shovel. How much did she pay for the gloves?

6. Roy is putting a brick walkway around a rectangular rock garden. The garden is 6.5 m wide and 5.4 m long. The walkway is 1 m wide. How many square meters of brick does he need?

WRITER'S CORNER

7. Write a problem similar to Exercise 3.

Dividing Mixed Numbers

Find the quotient. Write the quotient in simplest form.

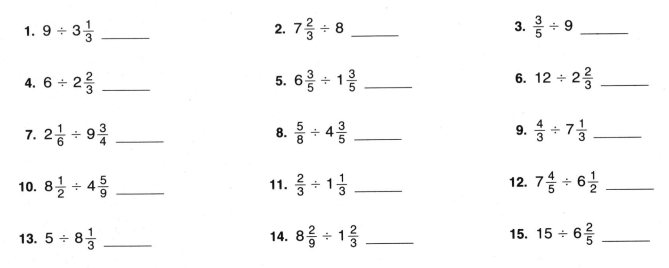

1. $9 \div 3\frac{1}{3}$ _____

2. $7\frac{2}{3} \div 8$ _____

3. $\frac{3}{5} \div 9$ _____

4. $6 \div 2\frac{2}{3}$ _____

5. $6\frac{3}{5} \div 1\frac{3}{5}$ _____

6. $12 \div 2\frac{2}{3}$ _____

7. $2\frac{1}{6} \div 9\frac{3}{4}$ _____

8. $\frac{5}{8} \div 4\frac{3}{5}$ _____

9. $\frac{4}{3} \div 7\frac{1}{3}$ _____

10. $8\frac{1}{2} \div 4\frac{5}{9}$ _____

11. $\frac{2}{3} \div 1\frac{1}{3}$ _____

12. $7\frac{4}{5} \div 6\frac{1}{2}$ _____

13. $5 \div 8\frac{1}{3}$ _____

14. $8\frac{2}{9} \div 1\frac{2}{3}$ _____

15. $15 \div 6\frac{2}{5}$ _____

Mixed Applications

16. Pierre bought a $64\frac{1}{2}$-oz bag of dog food. He feeds his dog $10\frac{3}{4}$ oz at each serving. How many servings are in each bag of dog food?

_____

17. Hulda has a $6\frac{2}{3}$-ft length of rope. She wants to cut it into 4 equal lengths. How long will each length of rope be?

_____

MATH CONNECTION

Compare. Write = or ≠ .

18. $\left(\frac{7}{8} \times \frac{4}{5}\right) \times 1\frac{3}{4}$ ◯ $\frac{7}{8} \times \left(\frac{4}{5} \times 1\frac{3}{4}\right)$

19. $\left(\frac{7}{8} \div \frac{4}{5}\right) \div 1\frac{3}{4}$ ◯ $\frac{7}{8} \div \left(\frac{4}{5} \div 1\frac{3}{4}\right)$

20. $3\frac{2}{3} \times \left(\frac{3}{7} \times \frac{9}{11}\right)$ ◯ $\left(3\frac{2}{3} \times \frac{3}{7}\right) \times \frac{9}{11}$

21. $3\frac{2}{3} \div \left(\frac{3}{7} \div \frac{9}{11}\right)$ ◯ $\left(3\frac{2}{3} \div \frac{3}{7}\right) \div \frac{9}{11}$

22. How does the Associative Property apply to multiplication and division with fractions and mixed numbers? Explain.

_____

Equations with Fractions

Solve the equation. Check your solution.

1. $n - \frac{1}{2} = 4\frac{1}{2}$

_____

2. $q + \frac{1}{4} = 5\frac{3}{4}$

_____

3. $6 = a + 2\frac{1}{3}$

_____

4. $w - 5\frac{4}{5} = 9\frac{3}{10}$

_____

5. $\frac{3}{4}x = 6$

_____

6. $\frac{b}{\frac{5}{6}} = \frac{2}{3}$

_____

7. $10 = 2\frac{1}{4}t$

_____

8. $5\frac{1}{6} = t + 2\frac{1}{3}$

_____

9. $\frac{z}{4} = 10\frac{3}{8}$

_____

10. $9r = 15\frac{1}{2}$

_____

11. $\frac{h}{\frac{1}{4}} - 2\frac{1}{2} = 10$

_____

12. $\frac{k}{3} - \frac{1}{2} = 12$

_____

Mixed Applications

Solve. Write an equation for Exercise 13.

13. Rod earned $60 in one week working for a lawn-care service. He worked for $12\frac{1}{2}$ hr. How much did he earn per hour?

_____

_____

14. Find the pattern in this sequence. Then write the next three terms in the sequence.

$5, 2\frac{1}{2}, 1\frac{1}{4}, \ldots$

_____

_____

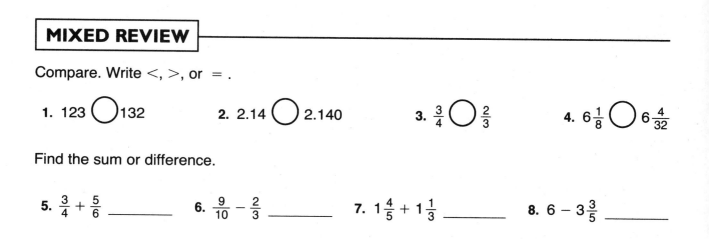

MIXED REVIEW

Compare. Write $<$, $>$, or $=$.

1. 123 $\bigcirc$ 132

2. 2.14 $\bigcirc$ 2.140

3. $\frac{3}{4}$ $\bigcirc$ $\frac{2}{3}$

4. $6\frac{1}{8}$ $\bigcirc$ $6\frac{4}{32}$

Find the sum or difference.

5. $\frac{3}{4} + \frac{5}{6}$ _____

6. $\frac{9}{10} - \frac{2}{3}$ _____

7. $1\frac{4}{5} + 1\frac{1}{3}$ _____

8. $6 - 3\frac{3}{5}$ _____

Decimals for Fractions

Write a decimal for the fraction or mixed number.

1. $\frac{3}{4}$ _____

2. $\frac{7}{10}$ _____

3. $\frac{7}{20}$ _____

4. $\frac{9}{32}$ _____

5. $\frac{7}{50}$ _____

6. $\frac{2}{5}$ _____

7. $\frac{5}{16}$ _____

8. $\frac{13}{50}$ _____

9. $\frac{5}{8}$ _____

10. $1\frac{3}{4}$ _____

11. $\frac{3}{25}$ _____

12. $\frac{17}{20}$ _____

13. $\frac{7}{16}$ _____

14. $\frac{3}{11}$ _____

15. $\frac{7}{18}$ _____

16. $2\frac{5}{9}$ _____

17. $\frac{3}{40}$ _____

18. $3\frac{1}{8}$ _____

19. $\frac{11}{30}$ _____

20. $\frac{2}{15}$ _____

Compare. Write $<$, $>$, or $=$.

21. $1.2 \bigcirc 1\frac{2}{5}$

22. $\frac{3}{4} \bigcirc 0.7$

23. $0.5 \bigcirc \frac{1}{2}$

24. $0.8 \bigcirc \frac{3}{5}$

25. $1\frac{2}{3} \bigcirc 1.6$

26. $4\frac{1}{2} \bigcirc 4.50$

27. $0.25 \bigcirc \frac{1}{25}$

28. $8.6 \bigcirc 8\frac{5}{6}$

Mixed Applications

29. Ed typed $4\frac{7}{8}$ pages of an office report. Write as a decimal the number of pages Ed typed.

_____

30. Kamaria completed a freestyle event in $2\frac{3}{5}$ min and a butterfly event in $2\frac{2}{3}$ min. Write as a decimal each event time. Which event was completed in the least time?

_____

MATH CONNECTION

31. Study your completed Exercises 1–30. Write a rule for predicting which fractions will have terminating decimals. (HINT: Factor the denominators.)

_____

_____

Fractions for Decimals

Write a fraction in simplest form or a mixed number for the decimal.

1. 0.8 _____   **2.** 0.12 _____   **3.** 0.7 _____   **4.** 0.05 _____

5. 0.075 _____   **6.** 0.45 _____   **7.** 0.25 _____   **8.** 0.020 _____

9. 4.5 _____   **10.** 3.94 _____   **11.** 5.24 _____   **12.** 8.36 _____

13. $0.\overline{1}$ _____   **14.** $0.\overline{45}$ _____   **15.** $0.1\overline{3}$ _____   **16.** $1.\overline{10}$ _____

17. 3.4 _____   **18.** 0.82 _____   **19.** $0.\overline{27}$ _____   **20.** $1.\overline{8}$ _____

Write in order from least to greatest.

21. $\frac{1}{3}$, 0.3, $\frac{2}{5}$

22. $0.\overline{8}$, $\frac{5}{6}$, $\frac{7}{8}$, $\frac{3}{4}$

23. $\frac{1}{2}$, 0.4, $\frac{6}{11}$, $0.\overline{5}$

_____   _____   _____

24. 0.38, $\frac{1}{4}$, $\frac{1}{3}$, 0.45

25. $1.\overline{2}$, 1.2, $1\frac{2}{7}$, $1\frac{1}{4}$

26. 0.125, $\frac{3}{25}$, $\frac{2}{9}$, $0.\overline{1}$

_____   _____   _____

Mixed Applications

27. A bag of sunflower seeds weighs 0.35 lb. Write the weight as a fraction.

28. Anica said she picked up 10.3125 lb of aluminum cans. Bertha said that she picked up $10\frac{1}{3}$ lb of cans. Who picked up more aluminum cans?

_____   _____

MATH CONNECTION

A decimal in which a pattern may occur but no group of decimals repeats is called a nonterminating, nonrepeating decimal.

29. Write a decimal that does not terminate or repeat.

_____

Problem Solving
Choose a Strategy

Mixed Applications ➤ **STRATEGIES**
- Write an Equation • Work Backward
- Guess and Check • Draw a Diagram
- Find a Pattern • Solve a Simpler Problem

Choose a strategy and solve.

1. Tony had some old comic books. He gave 8 to his brother and 3 to his sister. Then he divided the remaining comic books equally among himself and 2 friends. Tony ended up with 16 comic books for himself. How many comic books did he have to start?

_____

2. Five girls ran a cross-country track meet. Barbara came in first. Georgia came in last. Showanda finished ahead of Anita, and Greta finished just behind Anita. Which girl came in second?

_____

3. A math test had 15 problems worth 4 points each and 4 problems worth 10 points each. Juan solved 12 problems correctly for a total of 66 points. How many problems of each kind did he solve correctly?

_____

4. While on vacation Mikhail caught 1 fish on the first day. After that he caught 2 more fish each day than on the previous day. How many fish had he caught after the tenth day?

_____

5. Bobbie Jo planted 6 fewer than twice the number of seedlings that Marge planted. Bobbie Jo planted 26 seedlings. How many seedlings did Marge plant?

_____

6. Steve had 15 gray socks and 21 blue socks mixed together in a drawer. Without looking, how many socks would he have to pull from the drawer to be sure of getting a matching pair?

_____

WRITER'S CORNER

7. Write a word problem that can be solved by either of two different strategies. Identify the strategies.

_____

_____

_____

Basic Ideas in Geometry

Match one or more names from the list below with each figure in Exercises 1–4.

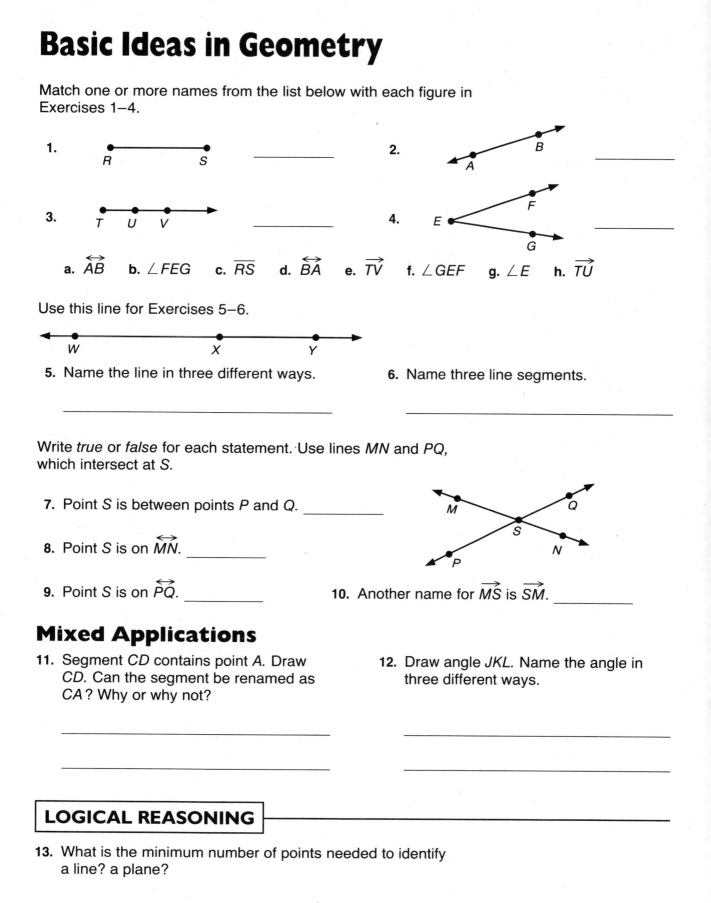

1. R •————————• S _____

2. _____

3. T • U • V •————▶ _____

4. _____

a. $\overleftrightarrow{AB}$ b. $\angle FEG$ c. $\overline{RS}$ d. $\overleftrightarrow{BA}$ e. $\overrightarrow{TV}$ f. $\angle GEF$ g. $\angle E$ h. $\overrightarrow{TU}$

Use this line for Exercises 5–6.

W •   X •   Y •

5. Name the line in three different ways.

_____

6. Name three line segments.

_____

Write *true* or *false* for each statement. Use lines *MN* and *PQ*, which intersect at *S*.

7. Point *S* is between points *P* and *Q.* _____

8. Point *S* is on $\overleftrightarrow{MN}$. _____

9. Point *S* is on $\overleftrightarrow{PQ}$. _____

10. Another name for $\overrightarrow{MS}$ is $\overrightarrow{SM}$. _____

Mixed Applications

11. Segment *CD* contains point *A*. Draw *CD*. Can the segment be renamed as *CA*? Why or why not?

_____

_____

12. Draw angle *JKL*. Name the angle in three different ways.

_____

_____

LOGICAL REASONING

13. What is the minimum number of points needed to identify a line? a plane?

_____

Angles and Angle Pairs

Find the missing measures.

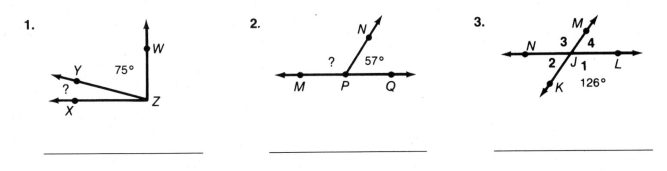

1.

2.

3.

_____   _____   _____

Draw the angle that is the complement and the angle that is the
supplement of the angle with the given measure.

4. 30°   5. 85°   6. 25°   7. 78°

Mixed Applications

The legs of a picnic bench form the given
angles. Use the figure for Exercises 8
and 9.

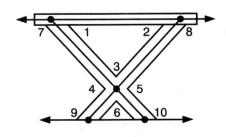

8. The measure of ∠ 3 is 72°. What are
   the measures of ∠ 4, ∠ 6, and ∠ 5?

9. Name two pairs of supplementary
   angles.

_____   _____

_____   _____

_____   _____

LOGICAL REASONING

10. True or false: ∠A is congruent to ∠B. If ∠A is acute,

   then ∠B is acute. _____

Constructing Congruent Segments and Angles

Construct a figure congruent to the given figure.

1.

2.

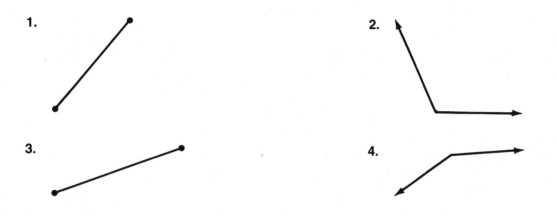

3.

4.

Draw the figure, using a ruler and a protractor. Then use the figure to construct a congruent figure, using a compass and a straightedge.

5. a 6-cm line segment

6. a 120° angle

Mixed Applications

7. Construct triangle ABC by constructing line segments and an angle congruent to the figures shown.

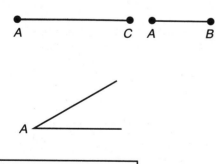

8. The measure of an angle is 40° more than the measure of its supplement. Find the measure of the angle and its supplement.

_____

9. The square of twice a number is equal to the number, taken to the third power, minus the number squared.

What is the number? _____

Exploring Parallel Lines and Transversals

Use the figure to find the measure of the given angle.

1. m∠2 = _____

2. m∠3 = _____

3. m∠4 = _____

4. m∠5 = _____

5. m∠6 = _____

6. m∠8 = _____

Tell whether the lines appear to be parallel or perpendicular.

7. _____

8. _____

9. _____

10. _____

Use the figure at the right for Exercises 11–19.

Name the corresponding angles.

11. ∠1 and _____

12. ∠2 and_____

13. ∠3 and _____

14. ∠4 and_____

15. Name four pairs of vertical angles.

_____

Name the alternate interior angles.

16. ∠4 and _____

17. ∠3 and_____

Name the alternate exterior angles.

18. ∠1 and _____

19. ∠2 and _____

LOGICAL REASONING

Tell whether the labeled lines are parallel.

20. 115° / 66° _____

21. 71° / 109° _____

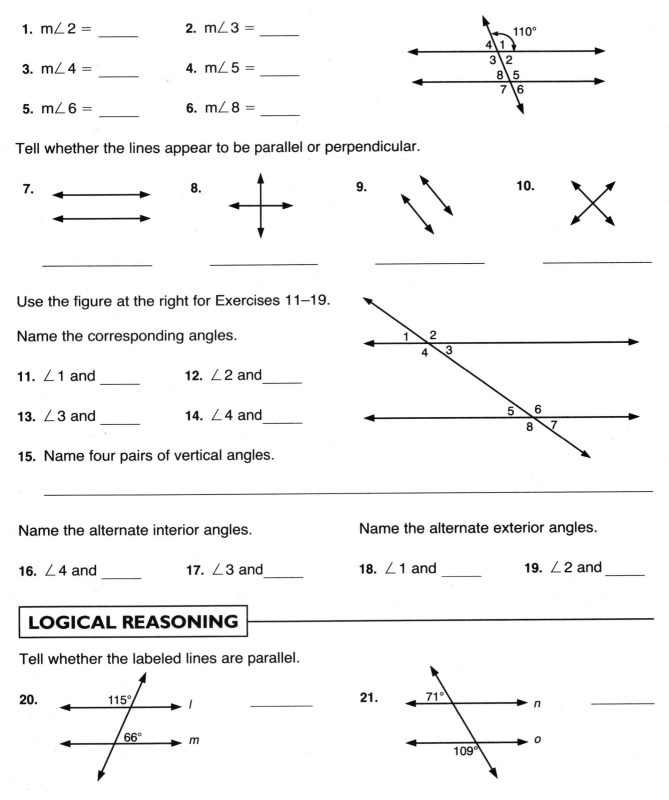

46

Constructing Parallel and Perpendicular Lines

Construct the following figures.

1. A line through point A perpendicular to $\overleftrightarrow{PQ}$.

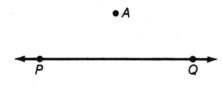

2. A line through point A parallel to $\overleftrightarrow{PQ}$.

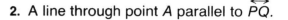
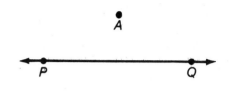

Mixed Applications

3. Construct two lines, one through point D, the other through point E, that are parallel to $\overleftrightarrow{AB}$. What is the relationship between the line through point D and the line through point E?

4. Construct a line through point P forming $\angle 2$ such that $\angle 1 \cong \angle 2$ and $\angle 1$ and $\angle 2$ are corresponding angles. What is the relationship between $\overleftrightarrow{AB}$ and the constructed line through point P?

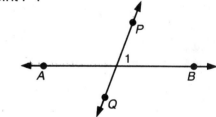

_____

_____

MIXED REVIEW

Write as a fraction in simplest form.

1. $\frac{12}{60}$ _____

2. $\frac{15}{45}$ _____

3. $\frac{18}{72}$ _____

4. $\frac{12\frac{1}{2}}{100}$ _____

Solve the equation.

5. $n + 99 = 109$

6. $n - 8 = 56$

7. $4n = 196$

8. $\frac{n}{8} = 5$

_____

_____

_____

_____

Exploring Bisecting Segments and Angles

Bisect the figures.

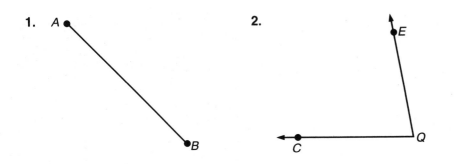

1. A

2. E
   C
   Q

3. Q
   R   S

Draw the figures using a ruler and a protractor. Construct bisectors using a compass and a straightedge.

4. a 5-cm line segment

5. a 96° angle

Mixed Applications

6. A painting is 36 in. wide. Mark wants the painting to be centered on a wall that is 144 in. wide. How much wall space will be left on each side of the painting?

_____

7. Ray *EF* bisects ∠*DEG*. m∠*DEF* = 43°. What is m∠*DEG*?

_____

LOGICAL REASONING

8. Stu uses a compass and a straightedge to bisect $\overline{AB}$. He places the point of the compass on point A, opens the compass, and draws an arc that intersects $\overline{AB}$. He places the point of the compass on point B, opens the compass, and draws another arc that intersects $\overline{AB}$. Stu realizes that the arcs do not intersect each other. What is his mistake?

_____

Problem-Solving Strategy

Find a Pattern

Choose the figure that completes the pattern.

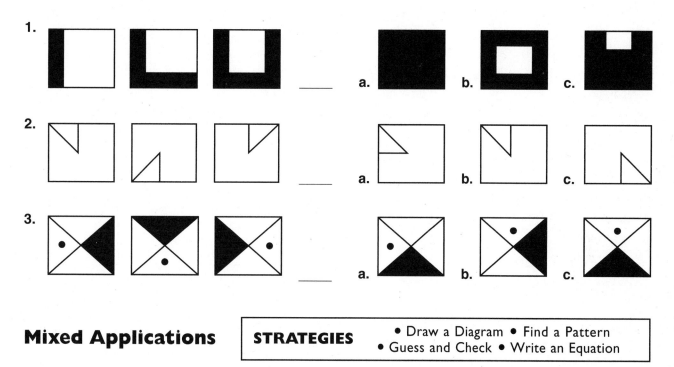

1.
   _____ a. b. c.

2.
   _____ a. b. c.

3.
   _____ a. b. c.

Mixed Applications

STRATEGIES • Draw a Diagram • Find a Pattern • Guess and Check • Write an Equation

Choose a strategy and solve.

4. Draw the figure that completes the pattern.

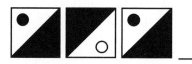

_____

5. Two three-digit numbers are between 300 and 500. For each number the sum of the digits is 12, and the sum of the hundreds digit and the ones digit equals the tens digit. Find the numbers.

_____

WRITER'S CORNER

6. Write a problem involving a pattern of three tiles that repeats after the third tile.

_____

_____

_____

_____

Polygons

Find the sum of the measures of the angles for each polygon.

1. triangle _____

2. 9-sided polygon _____

3. 14-sided polygon _____

4. 16-sided polygon _____

5. 22-sided polygon _____

6. 40-sided polygon _____

Tell the total number of diagonals each polygon can have.

7. 9-sided polygon _____

8. 12-sided polygon _____

9. 18-sided polygon _____

Draw the lines of symmetry for each quadrilateral.

10.   **11.**   **12.**   **13.**

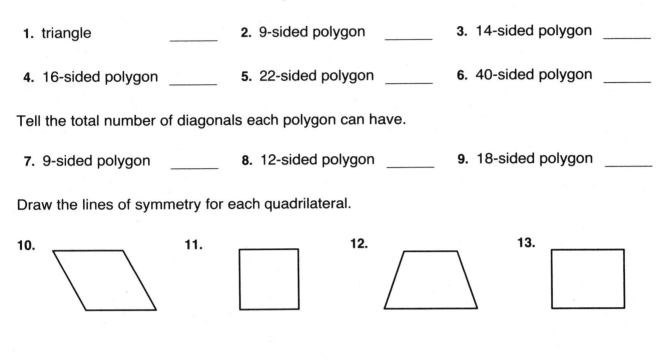

14. Look back at Exercises 10–13. Which quadrilaterals have a point of rotation for a rotation of 90°? for a rotation of 180°?

_____

Mixed Applications

15. In rhombus *ABCD,* the length of $\overline{AB}$ is 12 cm. Find the length of $\overline{CD}$.

16. The measure of one angle in a parallelogram is 135°. Find the measures of the other three angles.

_____

_____

LOGICAL REASONING

Write *true* or *false* for each statement.

17. If it is a rhombus, it is a quadrilateral. _____

18. If it is a rectangle, it is a parallelogram. _____

19. If it is a square, it is not a rectangle. _____

20. If it is a rhombus, it is a parallelogram. _____

Exploring Triangles

Use the figure for Exercises 1–11.

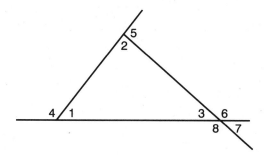

Tell which two angle measures have a sum equal to the measure of the given angle.

1. ∠4 _____   2. ∠5 _____   3. ∠8 _____

Find the indicated angle measure.

4. m∠3 = 40°, and m∠2 = 75°. Find m∠1.   _____

5. m∠1 = 50°, and m∠2 = 70°. Find m∠6.   _____

6. m∠1 = 45°, and m∠3 = 35°. Find m∠5.   _____

7. m∠2 = 74°, and m∠3 = 41°. Find m∠4.   _____

8. m∠4 = 135°, and m∠2 = 70°. Find m∠3.   _____

9. m∠8 = 143°, and m∠1 = 67°. Find m∠2.   _____

10. m∠5 = 118°, and m∠3 = 38°. Find m∠1.   _____

11. In the triangle, m∠1 = 62°, m∠2 = 78°, and m∠3 = 40°.
    Find m∠4 + m∠5 + m∠6.   _____

WRITER'S CORNER

12. What generalization can you make about the sum of the measures of the exterior angles of a triangle?

_____

_____

Congruent Polygons

1. Quadrilateral *ABCD* ≅ quadrilateral *MNOP.* Name the corresponding congruent sides and angles.

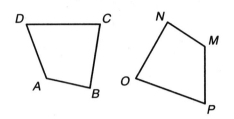

_____

_____

The polygons in each of Exercises 2–5 are congruent. Find *a*, *b*, and *c*.

2.

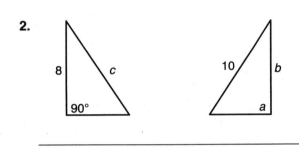

_____

3.

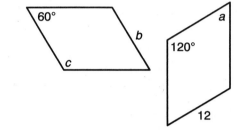

_____

4.

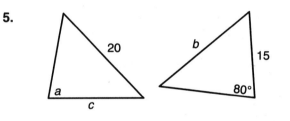

_____

5.

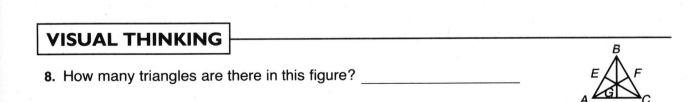

_____

Mixed Applications

6. Triangles *ABC* and *DEF* have corresponding congruent angles. Are the triangles necessarily congruent? Explain.

_____

_____

7. A diagonal divides quadrilateral *ABCD* into two triangles that are congruent. Identify quadrilateral *ABCD.*

_____

_____

| VISUAL THINKING |

8. How many triangles are there in this figure? _____

Constructing Congruent Triangles

Use the indicated rule to construct a triangle congruent to the given triangle.

1. SSS

2. SAS

3. ASA

Each pair of triangles is congruent. Find the missing measures.

4.

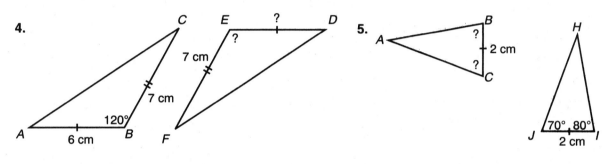

5.

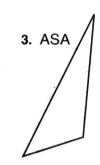

_____

_____

Mixed Applications

6. Two cabins are located at points *A* and *B* on either side of a lake. To find the distance *AB* between the cabins, Mika measures the distances *PA, PB, PC,* and *PD.* How will Mika use this information to find *AB*?

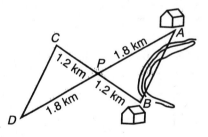

_____

_____

_____

| **LOGICAL REASONING** |

7. In quadrilateral *PQRS*, $\overline{SQ}$ bisects ∠ *PSR* to form triangle *PSQ* and triangle *RSQ*. $\overline{PS} \cong \overline{RS}$. Are the two triangles congruent? Why or why not?

_____

_____

53

Exploring Circles

Name the polygon formed when chords connect adjacent endpoints of the arcs. Find the arc measure in degrees.

1.

2.

3.

_____   _____   _____

4.

5.

6.

_____   _____   _____

Mixed Applications

Use the figure for Exercises 7–9. $\overleftrightarrow{AB} \parallel \overleftrightarrow{MN}$.

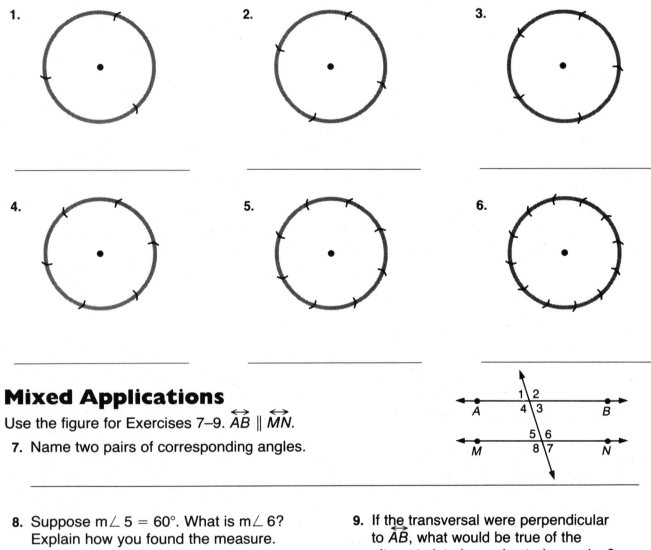

7. Name two pairs of corresponding angles.

_____

8. Suppose m∠ 5 = 60°. What is m∠ 6? Explain how you found the measure.

_____

9. If the transversal were perpendicular to $\overleftrightarrow{AB}$, what would be true of the alternate interior and exterior angles?

_____

MIXED REVIEW

Multiply or divide. Write the answer in simplest form.

1. $\frac{3}{5} \times \frac{9}{4}$ _____

2. $8 \div \frac{4}{5}$ _____

3. $\frac{9}{14} \div 1$ _____

4. $\frac{1}{3} \times \frac{15}{19}$ _____

5. $\frac{3}{8} \div \frac{6}{11}$ _____

6. $\frac{1}{2} \times \frac{6}{15}$ _____

7. $\frac{9}{10} \times \frac{5}{8}$ _____

8. $\frac{14}{15} \div 2$ _____

Problem Solving
Making Decisions

The Washingtons decided to add a room to the house. They asked three different builders to prepare an estimate of the total cost. The builders also indicated how they wished to be paid.

Choice 1 Hanson Construction

Estimate: $17,000
Terms of Payment: $1,000 on signing the construction contract. $16,000 to be paid one month after the construction is completed.

Choice 2 Walsh Homes

Estimate: $19,000
Terms of Payment: $2,500 on signing the construction contract. Forty-eight equal monthly payments plus a monthly interest charge of $90.78.

Choice 3 Stone Builders

Estimate: $18,000
Terms of Payment: $1,500 on signing the construction contract. Sixty equal monthly payments plus a monthly interest charge of $110.53.

Solve.

1. In Choice 2, how much will the Washingtons pay in interest over the 4 years?

_____

2. In Choice 2, how much will the Washingtons pay in all for the construction?

_____

3. In Choice 3, how much will the Washingtons pay in interest over the 5 years?

_____

4. In Choice 3, how much will the Washingtons pay in all for the construction?

_____

5. Suppose that the Washingtons have only $12,000 in savings. What choice does this eliminate?

_____

6. Suppose that the Washingtons want to completely pay for the construction before they take a vacation tour of the United States in 4 years. What choice does this eliminate?

_____

7. Name one advantage of Choice 2 over Choice 3.

_____

8. Name one advantage of Choice 3 over Choice 1.

_____

Ratios and Rates

Write the ratio in the form $\frac{a}{b}$.

1. 4 : 9 _____ **2.** 12 to 17 _____ **3.** 5 out of 8 _____ **4.** 53 : 100 _____

Write the ratio in simplest form.

5. $\frac{15}{35}$ _____ **6.** $\frac{12}{20}$ _____ **7.** $\frac{16}{30}$ _____ **8.** $\frac{25}{100}$ _____

Tell whether the ratio is equivalent to $\frac{2}{5}$. Write *yes* or *no*.

9. 4 : 10 _____ **10.** 6 : 12 _____ **11.** 10 to 25 _____ **12.** 50 to 20 _____

Write = or ≠ .

13. $\frac{3}{6}$ ◯ $\frac{1}{2}$ **14.** $\frac{4}{16}$ ◯ $\frac{12}{46}$ **15.** $\frac{8}{14}$ ◯ $\frac{4}{9}$ **16.** $\frac{45}{135}$ ◯ $\frac{9}{27}$

17. $\frac{20}{25}$ ◯ $\frac{15}{20}$ **18.** $\frac{32}{42}$ ◯ $\frac{17}{21}$ **19.** $\frac{40}{50}$ ◯ $\frac{4}{5}$ **20.** $\frac{6}{5}$ ◯ $\frac{18}{15}$

Write the unit rate.

21. $\frac{\$1.00}{10\ apples}$ _____ **22.** $\frac{\$1.50}{30\ oz\ of\ cereal}$ _____ **23.** $\frac{\$52}{4\ dinners}$ _____

Mixed Applications

24. Ana mixes concentrated shampoo and water in a 1 : 4 ratio. How many ounces of water does she mix with 4 oz of shampoo?

_____

25. Last year 66 people attended a computer workshop. This year 204 people attended. What is the ratio of last year's attendance to this year's? Write the ratio in simplest form.

_____

VISUAL THINKING ───────────────────────

Without counting all the sections, write the ratio of the shaded area to the total area. Write the ratio as $\frac{a}{b}$ in simplest form.

26.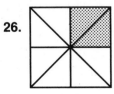

_____

27.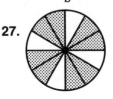

_____

28.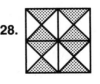

_____

56

Proportions

Write a proportion using two of the ratios.

1. $\frac{36}{46}$, $\frac{24}{32}$, $\frac{3}{4}$

2. $\frac{3}{8}$, $\frac{42}{104}$, $\frac{69}{184}$

3. 7 to 10, $\frac{280}{444}$, 70 : 111

_____   _____   _____

Write the equation that results when you cross multiply.

4. $\frac{1}{7} = \frac{30}{n}$

5. $\frac{6}{13} = \frac{n}{10}$

6. $\frac{n}{4} = \frac{8}{25}$

7. $\frac{200}{n} = \frac{100}{1}$

_____   _____   _____   _____

Solve the proportion.

8. $\frac{4}{5} = \frac{12}{n}$ _____

9. $\frac{1}{7} = \frac{n}{119}$ _____

10. $\frac{5}{1} = \frac{90}{n}$ _____

11. $\frac{4}{9} = \frac{n}{36}$ _____

12. $\frac{6}{7} = \frac{24}{n}$ _____

13. $\frac{7}{12} = \frac{n}{96}$ _____

14. $\frac{8}{3} = \frac{n}{27}$ _____

15. $\frac{5}{28} = \frac{45}{n}$ _____

16. $\frac{3}{3} = \frac{n}{200}$ _____

17. $\frac{5}{6} = \frac{n}{126}$ _____

18. $\frac{3}{10} = \frac{21}{n}$ _____

19. $\frac{n}{55} = \frac{5}{11}$ _____

20. $\frac{3}{8} = \frac{n}{0.48}$ _____

21. $\frac{1.8}{n} = \frac{12}{17}$ _____

22. $\frac{3}{7} = \frac{4.2}{n}$ _____

23. $\frac{4}{5} = \frac{n}{2.45}$ _____

Mixed Applications

24. In a certain classroom, the ratio of the number of soccer fans to the number of football fans was 3 : 2. There were 18 soccer fans. How many football fans were there?

_____

25. To paint the outside walls of their house, the Wagners mix blue paint and white paint in the ratio 2 : 3.5. How many gallons of white paint will they need to mix with 12 gal of blue paint?

_____

EVERYDAY MATH CONNECTION

A racing bicycle has a gear ratio of 38 to 19. This means that the front chain ring has 38 teeth and the rear sprocket has 19 teeth. Another racing bicycle has a 44-tooth chain ring.

26. How many teeth on the rear sprocket must the second racing bicycle have in order for the gear ratios of the two bicycles

to be the same? _____

Scale Drawings

Use the scale of 1 cm : 15 cm to find the missing dimension.

1. drawing: 4 cm

   actual: _____ cm

2. drawing: 9 cm

   actual: _____ cm

3. drawing: 22.5 cm

   actual: _____ cm

Use the scale of 15 cm : 1 cm to find the missing dimension.

4. drawing: 75 cm

   actual: _____ cm

5. drawing: _____ cm

   actual: 12.4 cm

6. drawing: 39 cm

   actual: _____ cm

Eartha completed a scale drawing of her school. Her scale was 1 in. : 60 ft. Measure the drawing. Then use the dimensions of the drawing and the scale to find the actual dimensions. Write both the drawing dimensions and the actual dimensions.

7. entire school

_____

8. cafeteria

_____

Mixed Applications

Solve. Use the scale of 1 in. : 50 ft.

9. The dimensions of a scale drawing of a library are 4 in. by 2 in. What are the actual dimensions of the library?

   _____

10. A stone walkway is being installed around the perimeter of the library. Each stone tile is 10 in. by 10 in. How many stone tiles are needed?

    _____

VISUAL THINKING

11. Use the scale of 1 cm : 1.5 m to make a scale drawing of a rectangle 9 m by 21 m.

Understanding Percent

Write as a percent.

1. 85 out of 100 _____

2. 42 out of 100 _____

3. 12 per 100 _____

4. 9 per 100 _____

5. 93 out of 100 _____

6. 79 per 100 _____

7. $\frac{3}{100}$ _____

8. $\frac{97}{100}$ _____

9. $\frac{49}{100}$ _____

10. 53 : 100 _____

11. $\frac{3}{20}$ _____

12. $\frac{1}{2}$ _____

13. $\frac{5}{25}$ _____

14. $\frac{2}{1}$ _____

15. $\frac{3}{4}$ _____

16. $\frac{9}{10}$ _____

17. $\frac{18}{50}$ _____

18. $\frac{4}{25}$ _____

19. $\frac{1}{20}$ _____

20. $\frac{167}{100}$ _____

21. $\frac{2}{5}$ _____

22. $\frac{17}{8}$ _____

Mixed Applications

23. The owner of Tourist T-shirts sold 80 T-shirts today. The owner calculated that $\frac{3}{4}$ of those T-shirts were size large. What percent of the T-shirts sold were size large?

   _____

24. The owner of Tourist T-shirts sells about $\frac{3}{5}$ of his T-shirts to teenagers. What percent of his T-shirts are sold to teenagers?

   _____

25. Last month $\frac{1}{10}$ of the T-shirts sold were size extra-large and $\frac{1}{8}$ were size extra-small. Were more extra-large or extra-small T-shirts sold last month?

   _____

26. During the month of July, $\frac{3}{20}$ of the T-shirts sold were size small and $\frac{10}{25}$ sold were size large. What percent of the T-shirts sold were neither small nor large?

   _____

VISUAL THINKING

27. What percent of the large square is shaded? Explain your reasoning.

   _____

   _____

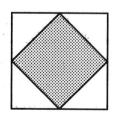

Connecting Percents, Decimals, and Ratios

Write as a decimal. Use mental math to solve.

1. 36% _____

2. 6% _____

3. 135% _____

4. 69% _____

5. 83% _____

6. 75% _____

7. 20% _____

8. 54% _____

Write as a percent. Use mental math to solve.

9. 0.85 _____

10. 0.3 _____

11. 1.74 _____

12. 0.145 _____

13. 1.25 _____

14. 0.08 _____

15. 0.51 _____

16. 0.0125 _____

Write as a ratio in simplest form.

17. 91% _____

18. 12% _____

19. 6% _____

20. 93% _____

21. 62% _____

22. 14% _____

23. 70% _____

24. 400% _____

Write as a percent. Use mental math, pencil and paper, or calculator to solve.

25. $\frac{3}{5}$ _____

26. $\frac{1}{3}$ _____

27. $\frac{1}{4}$ _____

28. $\frac{3}{20}$ _____

29. $\frac{3}{8}$ _____

30. $\frac{9}{20}$ _____

31. $\frac{4}{25}$ _____

32. $\frac{7}{1}$ _____

Mixed Applications

33. Crackle Corn Cereal contains 2% of the Recommended Daily Allowance (RDA) of protein. Write the percent as a decimal.

_____

34. Crackle Corn Cereal contains $\frac{2}{10}$ of the RDA of thiamin. Write the ratio as a percent.

_____

NUMBER SENSE

35. Crackle Corn Cereal contains twice the RDA of Vitamin C. Write the amount of Vitamin C as a percent and as a decimal.

_____

Exploring Percent Problems

1. Complete to solve the following problem:

   The Hat Hut sold 30 hats this morning. This was 40% of the number of hats it sold all day. How many hats did the Hat Hut sell today?

   Think: 40% of $\boxed{?}$ = _____

   $$\frac{40}{100} = \frac{30}{75}$$

   So, the Hat Hut sold _____ hats today.

Choose the correct percent problem for each word problem. Write **a**, **b**, or **c** at the right.

2. Bill had 50 baseball cards. He traded 20% of the cards with his friend Sam. How many baseball cards did he trade with Sam?

   a. ■% of 20 = 50   b. 20% of ■ = 50   c. 20% of 50 = ■   _____

3. Aimee had $10 in her wallet. She spent $4 on school supplies. What percent of her money did she spend on school supplies?

   a. ■% of 10 = 4   b. 4% of 10 = ■   c. 4% of ■ = 10   _____

4. Twelve students were chosen to act in a school play. This was 40% of the number of students who auditioned for the play. How many students auditioned for the play?

   a. ■% of 40 = 12   b. 40% of ■ = 12   c. 40% of 12 = ■   _____

5. Tom had $60 in his savings account. He withdrew 10% of his savings to pay a debt to his sister. How much money did he withdraw from his savings account?

   a. 10% of 60 = ■   b. 10% of ■ = 60   c. ■% of 60 = 10   _____

WRITER'S CORNER

6. Write a word problem that can be solved by the percent problem ■% of 85 = 51.

   _____

   _____

   _____

Finding a Percent of a Number

Find the percent of each number.

1. 75% of 92 _____

2. 150% of 75 _____

3. 15% of 650 _____

4. 115% of 720 _____

5. 27% of 487 _____

6. 3% of 87 _____

7. 0.3% of 63 _____

8. 62.5% of 640 _____

9. 21% of 87.3 _____

Solve.

10. Find 20% of $412.

_____

11. What number is 12% of 200?

_____

12. Find 4% of 800.

_____

13. Find 300% of 187.

_____

14. 5% of 10 is what number?

_____

15. Find 0.5% of 120.

_____

Complete. Write $<$, $>$, or $=$.

16. (75% of 40) + (25% of 40) $\bigcirc$ 100% of 40

17. (50% of 100) + (50% of 20) $\bigcirc$ 100% of 120

Mixed Applications

18. Northwind Airlines expects to have only 15% of its fleet of 80 jetliners under repair at any given time. How many jetliners would undergo repairs at any given time?

_____

19. Mr. Roe was notified that his automobile insurance would decrease by 4% starting next month because of his safe driving record. His current insurance premium is $624.00 per year. What is the amount of his premium decrease?

_____

MIXED REVIEW

Write as a ratio in simplest form.

1. 60% _____

2. 24% _____

3. 2% _____

4. 125% _____

5. 6% _____

6. 40% _____

7. 100% _____

8. 350% _____

Finding the Percent
One Number Is of Another

Find the percent.

1. What percent of 36 is 12? _____

2. What percent of 56 is 42? _____

3. 48 is what percent of 60? _____

4. 9 is what percent of 60? _____

5. What percent of 42 is 14? _____

6. 90 is what percent of 120? _____

7. 26 is what percent of 39? _____

8. What percent of 72 is 18? _____

9. What percent of 80 is 20? _____

10. What percent of 76 is 95? _____

11. What percent of 120 is 15? _____

12. 12 is what percent of 40? _____

13. 30 is what percent of 80? _____

14. What percent of 15 is 7? _____

15. What percent of 72 is 36? _____

16. 96 is what percent of 48? _____

17. What percent of 75 is 15? _____

18. What percent of 110 is 44? _____

19. 32 is what percent of 10? _____

20. What percent of 700 is 175? _____

Mixed Applications

21. Magic Smith made 70 free throws out of 105 attempts during the basketball season. What percent of the attempted free throws did he make?

22. In Luis's stamp collection, $\frac{3}{4}$ of the stamps are foreign. Of his foreign stamps, $\frac{1}{2}$ are French. What fraction of Luis's collection are the French stamps?

WRITER'S CORNER

23. Write a percent word problem that can be solved using the ratio $\frac{146}{365}$.

Finding the Number When the Percent Is Known

Find the number.

1. 85% of what number is 68? _____

2. 24 is 15% of what number? _____

3. 136.8 is 19% of what number? _____

4. 37% of what number is 74? _____

5. 0.6% of what number is 1.14? _____

6. 96% of what number is 192? _____

7. 145 is 58% of what number? _____

8. 0.25 is 0.05% of what number? _____

9. 4% of what number is 26.8? _____

10. 130% of what number is 75.4? _____

11. 24.6 is 24% of what number? _____

12. 75% of what number is 75? _____

13. 84% of what number is 210? _____

14. 0.98 is 35% of what number? _____

15. 5 is 0.2% of what number? _____

16. 35% of what number is 43.75? _____

17. 56% of what number is 39.2? _____

18. 11% of what number is 24.2? _____

Mixed Applications

19. By next year, 2,125 students are expected to be enrolled in a county's middle schools. This is 25% of the total student population. What is the total student population?

20. On a business trip, Ms. Rupp drove 4.25 hr on Monday, 6.75 hr on Tuesday, 5.50 hr on Wednesday, 7 hr on Thursday, and 6.75 hr on Friday. What is the total number of hours that Ms. Rupp drove?

_____

_____

MIXED REVIEW

Solve the proportion.

1. $\frac{1}{10} = \frac{12}{n}$ _____

2. $\frac{2}{3} = \frac{n}{9}$ _____

3. $\frac{4}{n} = \frac{20}{250}$ _____

Find the percent of each number.

4. 25% of 90 _____

5. 10% of 87.2 _____

6. 3% of 42 _____

Estimating Percents

Choose the best estimate. Write **a, b,** or **c.**

1. 20% of 49 _____
   a. 20% of 40
   b. 20% of 30
   c. 20% of 50

2. 25% of $81.25 _____
   a. 25% of $80
   b. 25% of $90
   c. 25% of $70

3. 150% of $41.50 _____
   a. $40
   b. $60
   c. $80

Write the common ratio that is nearly equivalent to each percent.

4. 32% _____

5. 78% _____

6. 65% _____

7. 89% _____

Estimate the percent.

8. $\frac{42}{160}$ _____

9. 88 : 180 _____

10. 14 out of 18 _____

11. 82 of 123 is about what percent?

_____

12. 147 is about what percent of 300?

_____

Estimate the number.

13. 25% of what number is 69?

_____

14. 50% of what number is 797?

_____

Mixed Applications

15. On a certain day, 112 of the 330 students brought their lunch to school. Estimate what percent of the students brought their lunch.

_____

16. The number of flower seeds planted this year is a multiple of 8 and also a multiple of 7. The number of seeds planted is between 70 and 120. How many seeds were planted this year?

_____

NUMBER SENSE

17. Using the signs + and − , complete the number sentence.

10% of 240 ☐ 25% of 180 ☐ 110% of 50 is 14.

Exploring Percent of Increase and Decrease

1. Complete to solve the following problem:

   In 1990 an automobile dealer sold 800 new cars. In 1991 the dealer sold 600 new cars. What is the percent of decrease?

   Think: amount of decrease 800 − _____ = _____.

   Percent of decrease = $\dfrac{\text{amount of decrease}}{\text{original amount}} = \dfrac{\square}{800}$

   Percent of decrease = $\dfrac{1}{\square}$ = _____%

2. Find the percent of increase.
   amount of increase: 80
   original amount: 100

   _____

3. Find the percent of decrease.
   amount of decrease: 36
   original amount: 40

   _____

4. Find the percent of increase.
   amount of increase: 25
   original amount: 30

   _____

5. Find the percent of decrease.
   amount of decrease: $100
   original salary: $25,000

   _____

Solve.

6. In 1990, there were 20 convenience stores in a city. By 1991, there were 60 convenience stores in the city. What is the

   percent of increase? _____

LOGICAL REASONING

7. Windle County had 4,000 high school students in 1970 and 4,500 high school students in 1980. By 1990 the number of high school students had increased 50% over the 1970 number. How many more high school students did the county have in 1990 than in 1980?

   _____

Percent of Increase and Decrease

Find the percent of increase or decrease.

1. 1990 cost: $60
   1991 cost: $80

   _____

2. 1980 earnings: $30,000
   1990 earnings: $45,000

   _____

3. 1989 amount: 600
   1991 amount: 360

   _____

4. 1980 sales: 500
   1990 sales: 1,000

   _____

5. 1990 savings: $4,000
   1991 savings: $1,500

   _____

6. 1989 amount: 1,450
   1991 amount: 1,305

   _____

7. 1990 cost: $12,000
   1991 cost: $16,000

   _____

8. 1985 sales: 90
   1990 sales: 72

   _____

9. 1989 amount: 200
   1990 amount: 230

   _____

10. 1990 cost: $25.00
    1991 cost: $25.50

    _____

11. 1989 sales: 390
    1991 sales: 273

    _____

12. 1980 earnings: $1,580
    1990 earnings: $1,738

    _____

Mixed Applications

13. Last year Cindy built a gymnastics set for $50. This year it cost her $75 to build one. What is the percent of increase?

    _____

14. Last week an almanac cost $3.50. This week it is on sale for $2.80. What is the percent of decrease?

    _____

EVERYDAY MATH CONNECTION

Discount is the amount off the regular price of an item. Discount is often written as a percent of the regular price. The sale price is the difference between the regular price and the amount of discount.

The regular price of a new car is $9,872. The car is on sale at a 15% discount.

15. What is the amount of the discount?

    _____

16. What is the sale price?

    _____

Simple Interest

Find the interest.

1. $p = \$625$
$r = 6\%$ per year
$t = 2$ yr _____

2. $p = \$150$
$r = 8\%$ per year
$t = 2$ yr _____

3. $p = \$225$
$r = 5\%$ per year
$t = 3$ yr _____

4. $p = \$1,590$
$r = 7\%$ per year
$t = 4$ yr _____

5. $p = \$1,940$
$r = 3\%$ per year
$t = 1\frac{1}{2}$ yr _____

6. $p = \$630$
$r = 4\%$ per year
$t = 3$ yr _____

7. $p = \$450$
$r = 7\%$ per year
$t = 4$ yr _____

8. $p = \$940$
$r = 8\%$ per year
$t = 3$ mo _____

9. $p = \$380$
$r = 7\%$ per year
$t = 6$ mo _____

10. $p = \$1,050$
$r = 2\%$ per year
$t = 1\frac{1}{2}$ yr _____

11. $p = \$800$
$r = 6\%$ per year
$t = 1$ yr _____

12. $p = \$1,100$
$r = 3\%$ per year
$t = 9$ mo _____

Mixed Applications

13. Tina borrows \$4,000 for 2 yr. The bank charges 12% interest per year. How much interest must she pay? Find the total amount she must pay.

_____

14. Ellis borrows \$750 to buy a piano. The bank charges 8% interest per year. He will pay \$30 in interest. For how long does Ellis borrow the money?

_____

MIXED REVIEW

Estimate the number.

1. 11% of what number is 91?

_____

2. 25% of what number is 24?

_____

Estimate the percent.

3. $\frac{48}{98}$ _____

4. 31 : 120 _____

5. $\frac{110}{532}$ _____

Problem-Solving Strategy
Use Estimation

Estimate a 15% tip for each bill.

1. $18.35   **2.** $24.60   **3.** $5.74   **4.** $12.05

_____   _____   _____   _____

5. $31.99   **6.** $29.67   **7.** $21.04   **8.** $9.82

_____   _____   _____   _____

Use estimation to solve.

9. Gabriel and his four friends ate dinner at a restaurant. The total bill was $68. Gabriel wanted to leave a 15% tip. Estimate the amount of the tip.

10. The cost of a dinner for four was $46.00. This included the amount for a 15% tip. What was the amount of the dinner alone?

Mixed Applications ➤ **STRATEGIES**
- Guess and Check • Use a Formula
- Use Estimation • Draw a Diagram

Choose a strategy and solve.

11. Rose borrowed $8,000 for 6 yr at an interest rate of 8% per yr. How much did she pay in interest? What was the total amount she paid?

12. You enter a maze and walk 8 paces forward, turn right and walk 5 paces, turn right and walk 2 paces, turn left and walk 3 paces, turn left and walk 6 paces, turn left and walk 11 paces, turn left and walk 12 paces. How many paces are you from the entrance?

GEOGRAPHY CONNECTION

13. Lake Erie has an area of 9,910 square miles. The area of Great Bear Lake is about 20% greater than the area of Lake Erie. Estimate the area of Great Bear Lake.

Understanding Integers

Write an integer for each description.

1. 27° below zero _____

2. a deposit of $20 _____

3. a loss of 4 lb _____

Write the absolute value.

4. |⁻4| _____

5. |⁻55| _____

6. |143| _____

7. |0| _____

Write the opposite.

8. ⁻91 _____

9. ⁻234 _____

10. 145 _____

11. ⁻81 _____

12. biking east 3 km

_____

13. spending $25

_____

14. rising 5°C

_____

Compare. Write <, >, or = .

15. 10 ◯ 20

16. ⁻4 ◯ ⁻7

17. ⁻10 ◯ ⁻6

18. |5| ◯ |⁻5|

Order the integers from least to greatest.

19. 2, ⁻3, ⁻5, 3

_____

20. 17, ⁻17, ⁻5, ⁻2

_____

21. 2, 5, ⁻7, 4, ⁻10

_____

Mixed Applications

22. What two integers represent 20 degrees above zero and 20 degrees below zero?

_____

23. The change in temperature from noon to 6:00 P.M. was 5°C. The change in temperature from 6:00 P.M. to midnight was −8°C. Which time period had the greater change in temperature?

_____

SCIENCE CONNECTION

24. Zero degrees Celsius is equal to 273 degrees Kelvin. If zero degrees Kelvin is absolute zero, what integer would represent absolute zero on the Celsius scale?

_____

Adding Integers

Find the sum.

1. 4 + 3 ____

2. ⁻2 + ⁻5 ____

3. ⁻9 + 4 ____

4. 7 + ⁻2 ____

5. ⁻11 + 4 ____

6. ⁻4 + ⁻4 ____

7. 6 + ⁻3 ____

8. 3 + ⁻12 ____

9. 5 + ⁻3 ____

10. 12 + ⁻20 ____

11. 15 + ⁻4 ____

12. 40 + 5 ____

13. ⁻2 + 22 ____

14. ⁻7 + 7 ____

15. 13 + ⁻3 ____

16. 25 + ⁻33 ____

17. ⁻19 + ⁻4 ____

18. 12 + ⁻9 ____

19. ⁻21 + 21 ____

20. ⁻4 + 20 ____

21. 60 + ⁻8 ____

22. ⁻6 + 22 ____

23. ⁻23 + ⁻16 ____

24. 43 + ⁻26 ____

25. 126 + ⁻9 ____

26. ⁻102 + 88 ____

27. 28 + ⁻97 ____

28. ⁻154 + 6 ____

29. 7 + ⁻3 + 11 ____

30. 22 + ⁻5 + ⁻2 ____

31. ⁻18 + 4 + ⁻24 ____

32. (4 + ⁻16) + 12 ____

33. (⁻52 + 21) + 25 ____

34. 9 + (6 + ⁻14) ____

Mixed Applications

35. A diver is swimming at ⁻10 m. He then descends 3 m and rises 6 m. At what new level is the diver swimming?

_____

36. Yesterday 37½% of the customers in Mall Mart paid by credit card. If 582 customers paid by credit card, how many customers were there in all?

_____

37. Each term in a number sequence is 5 greater than the term before it. The first term is ⁻24. Write the next six terms in the sequence.

_____

38. The level of water in a pail has changed by ⁻7 in. from the original water level. If the original level was 23 in., what is the current level?

_____

NUMBER SENSE

39. The sum of two integers is ⁻23. If the sign of one integer is changed, the new sum will be ⁻3. What are the two integers? Which integer will have its sign changed?

_____

Subtracting Integers

Find the difference.

1. $4 - {}^-13$ _____

2. ${}^-3 - {}^-11$ _____

3. ${}^-17 - {}^-11$ _____

4. ${}^-8 - {}^-2$ _____

5. ${}^-32 - {}^-54$ _____

6. ${}^-30 - 12$ _____

7. $22 - 14$ _____

8. ${}^-7 - {}^-12$ _____

9. ${}^-14 - {}^-30$ _____

10. ${}^-33 - {}^-22$ _____

11. $41 - {}^-22$ _____

12. $28 - 42$ _____

13. $32 - 24$ _____

14. $100 - {}^-2$ _____

15. ${}^-16 - 6$ _____

16. ${}^-3 - {}^-3$ _____

17. $11 - {}^-20$ _____

18. ${}^-74 - 44$ _____

19. $126 - 154$ _____

20. ${}^-35 - {}^-41$ _____

21. ${}^-41 - {}^-44$ _____

22. $7 - 35$ _____

23. $61 - {}^-61$ _____

24. $24 - 24$ _____

Compute.

25. ${}^-4 - {}^-2 - 7$ _____

26. ${}^-11 + 2 - 8$ _____

27. $({}^-7 + 3) - {}^-4$ _____

Mixed Applications

28. Lian is standing 20 ft above sea level. Mary is swimming 10 ft below sea level, or at ${}^-10$ ft. How much higher is Lian's position than Mary's?

_____

29. A diver is at ${}^-20$ m. The ocean floor is at ${}^-135$ m. If the diver rises 3 m, how far will he be from the ocean floor?

_____

30. The sum of two integers is ${}^-9$. When the smaller integer is subtracted from the larger integer, the difference is 1. What are the integers?

_____

31. At Multi Muffins, $\frac{1}{3}$ of the muffins sold are bran muffins. Of the bran muffins sold, $\frac{2}{5}$ have raisins. What fraction of the muffins sold are raisin bran muffins?

_____

MIXED REVIEW

Compare. Write $<$, $>$, or $=$.

1. $\frac{4}{5} \bigcirc \frac{3}{8}$

2. $3\frac{1}{4} \bigcirc \frac{33}{10}$

3. $\frac{7}{4} \bigcirc \frac{9}{8}$

4. $\frac{11}{7} \bigcirc 1\frac{1}{3}$

5. ${}^-10 \bigcirc 3$

6. ${}^-5 \bigcirc {}^-1$

7. $0 \bigcirc {}^-11$

8. $6 \bigcirc {}^-10$

Multiplying Integers

Find the product.

1. 8 · 4 _____

2. 16 · ⁻2 _____

3. ⁻13 · 6 _____

4. ⁻14 · 9 _____

5. 7 · ⁻3 _____

6. ⁻2 · 17 _____

7. 20 · ⁻6 _____

8. ⁻5 · 18 _____

9. ⁻18 · ⁻3 _____

10. 6 · ⁻15 _____

11. ⁻17 · ⁻9 _____

12. 9 · ⁻6 _____

13. 6 · 11 _____

14. 13 · ⁻3 _____

15. ⁻10 · ⁻5 _____

16. 14 · ⁻9 _____

17. ⁻17 · 4 _____

18. ⁻15 · ⁻8 _____

19. 9 · ⁻9 _____

20. 2 · ⁻18 _____

21. ⁻3 · ⁻8 _____

22. ⁻18 · ⁻8 _____

23. 16 · ⁻5 _____

24. 22 · ⁻10 _____

25. 30 · ⁻3 _____

26. ⁻25 · ⁻6 _____

27. 40 · ⁻3 _____

28. ⁻2 · ⁻2 · 2 _____

29. 4 · ⁻5 · ⁻2 _____

30. ⁻13 · 3 · ⁻2 _____

31. ⁻3 · 6 · 2 _____

32. ⁻18 · 2 · ⁻2 _____

33. 11 · ⁻3 · 6 _____

Mixed Applications

34. Erica has $40. She wants to buy 3 cans of blue paint for her bicycle. Paint costs $5 per can. How much money will she have left?

_____

35. The sum of two integers is ⁻1. The product of these integers is ⁻56. What are the integers?

_____

SCIENCE CONNECTION

36. Have you ever wondered how much food is used to produce your canned favorites in the supermarket? When food is cooked, it loses weight because water is removed. During processing, 500 pounds of a certain food loses 90 pounds of water. How many cans of prepared food are produced if each can holds 1 pound of food?

_____

Dividing Integers

Find the quotient.

1. $^-22 \div 2$ _____

2. $39 \div ^-13$ _____

3. $^-45 \div 9$ _____

4. $^-99 \div ^-3$ _____

5. $84 \div ^-7$ _____

6. $^-110 \div ^-5$ _____

7. $^-125 \div 5$ _____

8. $270 \div ^-9$ _____

9. $^-42 \div 6$ _____

10. $\dfrac{^-240}{^-20}$ _____

11. $\dfrac{560}{^-40}$ _____

12. $\dfrac{640}{^-80}$ _____

Compute.

13. $(^-99 \div 3) \cdot 2$ _____

14. $^-13 + (^-34 \div ^-2)$ _____

15. $90 - (99 \div 9)$ _____

16. $12 \cdot (39 \div ^-3)$ _____

17. $(^-86 \div ^-43) + 98$ _____

18. $(64 \div ^-8) \cdot 3$ _____

Mixed Applications

19. A water tank has a leak. The amount of water changes by $^-8$ gal per day. When the total change is $^-400$ gal, the water pump will stop working. In how many days will this happen?

_____

20. A rope is used to repair a broken swing. During the summer, the length of the rope changes by $^-2$ in. per week. How much shorter is the rope at the end of 12 weeks of summer?

_____

If N is any negative integer, P is any positive integer, and Z is zero, state whether the answer is P, N, or Z.

21. $(P \div N) + (N \cdot Z)$ _____

22. $(P \cdot N) \cdot (N \div N)$ _____

ART CONNECTION

23. Industries often lose money in wasting raw materials. Find out how much a ceramics company was losing every week from tile breakage. The raw materials for 1 day cost $2,000, and 10,000 floor tiles were produced. These tiles were then packaged 50 tiles per box and stored in a warehouse. Each day 4 boxes of tiles were broken during handling. How much money was lost for a 5-day working week?

_____

Properties of Integers

Name the property shown.

1. $^-13 + 3 = 3 + {}^-13$

   _____

2. $^-6 + 0 = {}^-6$

   _____

3. $10 \cdot ({}^-4 \cdot 3) = (10 \cdot {}^-4) \cdot 3$

   _____

4. $^-7 \cdot 1 = {}^-7$

   _____

5. $^-2 + 2 = 0$

   _____

6. $15 \cdot ({}^-6 + 4) = (15 \cdot {}^-6) + (15 \cdot 4)$

   _____

Use the properties to find each answer. Use mental math where possible.

7. $({}^-3 + 5) + {}^-6 = $ _____

8. $14 \cdot (10 + 7) = $ _____

9. $^-23 + 25 + 0 = $ _____

10. $^-13 + 20 + 13 + 13 = $ _____

11. $^-13 + 0 + 7 + {}^-4 = $ _____

12. $422 - 40 + 40 = $ _____

13. $62 + 13 - 13 - 55 = $ _____

14. $({}^-8 \cdot 13) + ({}^-8 \cdot 7) = $ _____

Mixed Applications

15. A fashion designer bought 3 pieces of cloth each 6 m long, 4 pieces each 10 m long, and 2 pieces each 5 m long. What is the total number of meters of cloth?

    _____

16. A writer wrote 30 lines on a page, erased 15 lines, added 12 lines, then erased 5 lines. How many lines were left on the page?

    _____

PHYSICAL EDUCATION CONNECTION

17. Mike jogs every day. If he jogs 3 mi a day for 5 days of the week and then twice that distance on Saturdays and Sundays, what is the total distance he jogs in a week?

    _____

Integers as Exponents

Write as an expression having a negative exponent.

1. $\frac{1}{5^1} = $ _____

2. $\frac{1}{10^7} = $ _____

3. $\frac{1}{8^3} = $ _____

4. $\frac{1}{100} = $ _____

5. $\frac{1}{2 \cdot 2 \cdot 2 \cdot 2 \cdot 2} = $ _____

6. $\frac{1}{64} = $ _____

7. $\frac{1}{27} = $ _____

8. $\frac{1}{1,000,000} = $ _____

9. $\frac{1}{25} = $ _____

Write as a fraction or a decimal.

10. $10^{-4} = $ _____

11. $10^{-7} = $ _____

12. $10^{-6} = $ _____

13. $2^{-5} = $ _____

14. $3^{-1} = $ _____

15. $10^{-1} = $ _____

16. $9^{-2} = $ _____

17. $5^{-3} = $ _____

18. $3^{-4} = $ _____

19. $10^{-2} = $ _____

20. $4^{-2} = $ _____

21. $11^{-2} = $ _____

22. $(^-6)^{-1} = $ _____

23. $(^-3)^{-3} = $ _____

24. $(^-5)^{-2} = $ _____

25. $(^-2)^{-6} = $ _____

26. $(^-12)^{-1} = $ _____

27. $(^-12)^{-2} = $ _____

Mixed Applications

Tell whether you would use an expression with a *positive exponent* or an expression with a *negative exponent* for Exercises 28–29.

28. The weight of a dust particle is about 0.0000001 g.

_____

29. Sound travels about 1,200,000 m per hour.

_____

LOGICAL REASONING

30. Consider the numbers $9,999^{-1}$, $9,999^{-2}$, $9,999^{-3}$, $9,999^{-4}$, and so on. Are any of these numbers negative? Explain your answer.

_____

_____

Exploring Products and Quotients of Powers

Write the addition or subtraction expression that will give you the exponent of the answer.

1. $9 \cdot 9^9$ _____

2. $10^4 \cdot 10^{-4}$ _____

3. $7^2 \div 7^{-3}$ _____

4. $4^{-9} \div 4^{-9}$ _____

5. $10^{-10} \div 10$ _____

6. $12^{-7} \div 12^{-2}$ _____

Write the product as one power.

7. $2^4 \cdot 2^6$ _____

8. $4^4 \cdot 4^5$ _____

9. $8^{10} \cdot 8$ _____

10. $14^{-7} \cdot 14$ _____

11. $9^{-5} \cdot 9^{-4}$ _____

12. $3^6 \cdot 3^{-5}$ _____

13. $7^{-10} \cdot 7^2$ _____

14. $6^8 \cdot 6^5$ _____

15. $(^-10)^{-3} \cdot (^-10)^8$ _____

16. $(^-5)^4 \cdot (^-5)^{-9}$ _____

17. $(^-6)^{-4} \cdot (^-6)^8 \cdot (^-6)^{-5}$ _____

Write the quotient as one power.

18. $4^4 \div 4^3$ _____

19. $10^6 \div 10$ _____

20. $12^2 \div 12$ _____

21. $8^{12} \div 8^{10}$ _____

22. $9^3 \div 9^{-6}$ _____

23. $11^{-7} \div 11^5$ _____

24. $3^{-2} \div 3^{-3}$ _____

25. $10^{-5} \div 10^{-8}$ _____

26. $2^{-6} \div 2^6$ _____

27. $(^-9)^0 \div (^-9)^{-9}$ _____

28. $(^-7)^{-10} \div (^-7)^0$ _____

29. $(4.2)^{-3} \div (4.2)^{-2}$ _____

SCIENCE CONNECTION

30. Medical research develops new drugs to treat diseases. Much of the research takes place in pharmaceutical laboratories. Suppose a researcher tests a prototype antibiotic on a certain strain of bacteria. If the antibiotic kills the bacteria at a rate of 7^{15} bacteria per second, how many bacteria would be killed after 7^{10} seconds?

_____

Scientific Notation

Write in scientific notation.

1. 12,000 _____

2. 57,000,000,000 _____

3. 0.00043 _____

4. 0.00000000876 _____

5. 0.0024 _____

6. 0.00000017 _____

7. 0.000009 _____

8. 80,450,000 _____

9. 6,300,000,000 _____

10. 0.0000006 _____

Write in standard form.

11. 4×10^5 _____

12. 5.7×10^3 _____

13. 9×10^6 _____

14. 5×10^2 _____

15. 3.3×10^7 _____

16. 9×10^{-4} _____

17. 6.4×10^{-2} _____

18. 2.3×10^3 _____

19. 9×10^5 _____

20. 5×10^{-7} _____

Mixed Applications

21. The width of a thin wire is 0.0000067 m. Write the number in scientific notation.

22. The number of rice seeds in a bag is 385,000,000. Write this number using the word *million*.

_____

_____

SCIENCE CONNECTION

23. Much biological research involves breeding plants. A research scientist estimates that a certain hybrid plant produces 12,500,000 grains of pollen and that the grains are 0.00092 in. long. Write these numbers in scientific notation.

_____

Problem Solving
Choose a Strategy

Mixed Applications → **STRATEGIES**   • Write an Equation   • Use Estimation   • Draw a Diagram   • Guess and Check

Choose a strategy and solve.

1. A submarine's position in the ocean was ⁻14 m. In 4 minutes, the submarine changed its position to ⁻66 m. What was the average change in position per minute?

   _____

2. Paul purchased a CD player and 5 CDs. The total he spent was $257.50, and the CD player cost $210. What was the average cost of each CD?

   _____

3. The high temperature in October was 77°F. What was the low temperature in December, if it was 84° less than the high in October?

   _____

4. The temperature in the morning was 45°F. The hottest temperature in the afternoon was 87°F. What was the average temperature increase during the 6 hours?

   _____

5. The Chungs went on vacation and used a total of 435 gal of gas. They used 30 gal more than 2 times as much gas to get to their destination as to get home. How much gas did they use to get home?

   _____

6. At the local computer store, there was a sale on computer disks. Brand A was on sale at $15 for a box of 10. Brand B was on sale at $19.60 for a box of 15. Which brand costs less per disk?

   _____

SCIENCE CONNECTION

7. Write a problem about an airplane changing altitude over a 1-minute period. Solve.

   _____

79

Rational Numbers

Write each rational number in the form $\frac{a}{b}$.

1. 0.5 _____

2. $^-2\frac{1}{3}$ _____

3. 4 _____

4. 2.6 _____

5. 0.8 _____

6. $^-3\frac{3}{4}$ _____

7. 2.25 _____

8. $1\frac{4}{5}$ _____

Compare. Write $<$, $>$, or $=$.

9. $\frac{1}{7}$ ◯ $\frac{-1}{7}$

10. $^-0.8$ ◯ 0.8

11. $\frac{3}{4}$ ◯ $\frac{4}{5}$

12. $^-1.5$ ◯ $\frac{3}{5}$

Write in order from least to greatest.

13. $^-2, \frac{1}{4}, ^-1\frac{2}{3}$

_____

14. $\frac{3}{4}, \frac{4}{7}, 1\frac{2}{3}, 2, 2.3$

_____

15. $^-1.3, ^-1\frac{1}{3}, \frac{3}{6}, \frac{2}{5}, \frac{2}{3}$

_____

16. $1.45, 1\frac{2}{5}, 2.7, 2\frac{3}{8}, 1$

_____

Mixed Applications

17. At 7:00 A.M., the temperature was $^-12.3$ F. At 8:00 A.M., it was $^-13.7$ F. At which time was it colder?

_____

18. First a U.S. submarine is 220.8 ft below sea level. Then its position changes to 221.3 ft below sea level. Did it descend or rise?

_____

SCIENCE CONNECTION

To convert temperatures from degrees Fahrenheit to degrees Celsius, subtract 32°, and multiply by $\frac{5}{9}$.

Find each temperature in degrees Celsius.

19. 50°F _____

20. 104°F _____

21. 0°F _____

Squares and Square Roots

Write *SR* if the first number is the square root of the second number, write *S* if it is the square, or write *N* if it is neither.

1. 9, 81

2. 15, 225

3. 169, 13

4. 125, ⁻5

5. 2, 4

_____   _____   _____   _____   _____

Find the square.

6. 3^2

7. 14^2

8. $(^-7)^2$

9. $(^-13)^2$

10. $(^-16)^2$

_____   _____   _____   _____   _____

11. $(0.6)^2$

12. $\left(\frac{4}{5}\right)^2$

13. $\left(\frac{-5}{12}\right)^2$

14. $\left(\frac{13}{6}\right)^2$

_____   _____   _____   _____

Find the two square roots of each number.

15. 121

16. 256

17. 196

18. 400

19. 900

_____   _____   _____   _____   _____

Find the square root.

20. $\sqrt{49}$

21. $^-\sqrt{81}$

22. $\sqrt{144}$

23. $^-\sqrt{64}$

24. $\sqrt{225}$

_____   _____   _____   _____   _____

Mixed Applications

25. The formula for the distance, *d*, an accelerating car can travel is $d = 5.6t^2$. How long (t) does the car take to travel 1,814.4 m?

_____

26. The backyard of a house is a square whose area is 900 m². How much fencing is needed to enclose the yard?

_____

NUMBER SENSE

27. Bob was thinking of a number between 5 and 15 that when squared and added to 23 equals the next number's square.

What is the number? _____

Finding Square Roots

Estimate to find the square root to the nearest tenth.

1. $\sqrt{89}$ _____

2. $\sqrt{123}$ _____

3. $\sqrt{20}$ _____

4. $^-\sqrt{61}$ _____

Find the square root to the nearest hundredth.

5. $\sqrt{3}$ _____

6. $\sqrt{17}$ _____

7. $^-\sqrt{34}$ _____

8. $\sqrt{87}$ _____

9. $\sqrt{124}$ _____

10. $\sqrt{111}$ _____

11. $\sqrt{0.04}$ _____

12. $^-\sqrt{0.21}$ _____

Find the square root to the nearest tenth when $a = 7$ and $b = 2$.

13. $\sqrt{a - b}$ _____

14. $\sqrt{a^2}$ _____

15. $\sqrt{b^2 + a}$ _____

Mixed Applications

The graph shows the positive square roots of the numbers from 1 to 50. Use the graph for Exercises 16–18.

16. What is the approximate square root of 50?

_____

17. What is the approximate square root of 30?

_____

18. Can you approximate the square root of 0.07? Explain.

_____

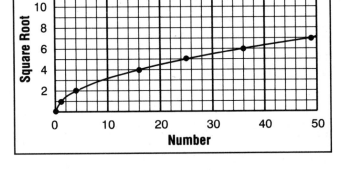

WRITER'S CORNER

19. Give one advantage and one disadvantage of using a graph to find square roots.

_____

_____

_____

Exploring Irrational Numbers

Complete the table. Then classify the number by placing an *x* in each appropriate column. The first exercise has been done.

		Real Number	Rational Number	Whole Number	Integer	Irrational Number
1.	210	x	x	x	x	
2.	312					
3.	⁻9.1					
4.	3.14159 . . .					
5.	$-\sqrt{13}$					
6.	⁻10					
7.	$6\frac{1}{3}$					
8.	$(0.39)^2$					
9.	7.21212 . . .					

10. Order the numbers in Exercises 1–9 from least to greatest.

_____

Find the positive square root. Then classify it as a real, a rational, a whole, an irrational number or an integer.

11. 49

12. 14

13. 0.18

14. 0.81

SCIENCE CONNECTION

15. In electronics, power is equal to the square of the voltage divided by the resistance of a circuit. If the power is equal to 7, which of these resistances will yield a rational-number voltage: 7, 14, 63, 4, 28?

$$p = \frac{v^2}{r}$$

Adding and Subtracting

Find the sum or difference.

1. $\frac{2}{3} + \frac{^-1}{3}$ _____

2. $\frac{^-3}{8} + \frac{4}{8}$ _____

3. $\frac{^-2}{9} + 3$ _____

4. $\frac{^-2}{5} + \frac{^-1}{5}$ _____

5. $\frac{2}{4} + \frac{^-3}{4}$ _____

6. $^-6 + \frac{^-4}{7}$ _____

7. $^-2.1 + {}^-4.1$

_____

8. $0.3 + {}^-0.9$

_____

9. $^-4.21 + {}^-7.12$

_____

10. $\frac{3}{4} - \frac{^-1}{3}$ _____

11. $\frac{^-6}{7} - \frac{^-1}{2}$ _____

12. $\frac{3}{13} - \frac{^-7}{8}$ _____

13. $\frac{^-4}{10} - \frac{^-3}{5}$ _____

14. $\frac{^-4}{11} - \frac{^-13}{22}$ _____

15. $\frac{^-5}{9} - \frac{^-3}{18}$ _____

16. $^-3.2 - {}^-7.4$

_____

17. $0.12 - {}^-8.63$

_____

18. $^-7.21 - {}^-12.4$

_____

19. $^-2.11 - {}^-6.9$

_____

20. $^-13.2 - {}^-6.41$

_____

21. $^-21.6 - 9.09$

_____

Mixed Applications

22. Marta is keeping track of how many dozen eggs she sells in a week. On Monday she had 3 dozen eggs to sell. By Wednesday she had gathered $2\frac{1}{2}$ dozen more from her hens. If by Friday, she had only 3 eggs left, how many had she sold during the week?

_____

23. Rainie kept track of the temperature during January. Her figures showed the average temperature for each of four weeks were 11.3°C, $^-$4.7°C, $^-$7.01°C, and $^-$21.6°C. What was the difference between the highest and lowest weekly average temperature?

_____

NUMBER SENSE

24. If you add $^-$5 to an integer and then subtract $^-$3 from that sum, is the result less than or greater than the original number?

_____

84

Problem-Solving Strategy
Make a Table

1. Randy, Paul, and Joe are members of the Air Force, Army, and Coast Guard. Paul isn't in the Coast Guard but can beat Randy at arm wrestling. Paul can't beat Joe at arm wrestling and Joe isn't in the Air Force. If the strongest is in the Army, who belongs to which force?

   _____

2. Chuck, Mary, Tai, and Tyrone play baseball. The pitcher is the tallest on the team and likes math. Mary is taller than Chuck, who likes science. The first baseman is the shortest on the team and likes music. Tyrone, who doesn't like math, is shorter than Tai who likes English. The shortstop likes science. The catcher likes English. Who plays which position?

   _____

   _____

Mixed Applications >	STRATEGIES	• Make a Table • Use Estimation • Write an Equation • Guess and Check

Choose a strategy and solve.

3. Jack is $\frac{2}{3}$ as old as his sister Janice. Janice was 14 years old seven years ago. Their cousin Dana is the sum of both their ages. How old is Dana now?

   _____

4. Zap tennis balls cost $118.45 for 200. Yellow brand tennis balls cost $23.12 for 45, and 115 White brand tennis balls cost $63.48. If you plan to buy 200 tennis balls, which brand would cost least? How much would you pay?

   _____

NUMBER SENSE

5. Three times a whole number is equal to one half the square of the number.

   What is the number? _____

Multiplying and Dividing

Find the product or quotient.

1. $\frac{2}{4} \cdot \frac{-1}{9}$ _____

2. $\frac{1}{5} \cdot \frac{3}{5}$ _____

3. $\frac{2}{7} \cdot \frac{-2}{3}$ _____

4. $\frac{-6}{9} \cdot \frac{8}{13}$ _____

5. $\frac{3}{6} \div \frac{-1}{2}$ _____

6. $\frac{-3}{9} \div \frac{2}{3}$ _____

7. $\frac{-1}{4} \div \frac{-4}{5}$ _____

8. $\frac{5}{12} \div \frac{-6}{7}$ _____

9. $^-2.7 \cdot 0.4$ _____

10. $^-11.4 \cdot 1.2$ _____

11. $^-5 \cdot {}^-0.2$ _____

12. $4.2 \div 0.21$ _____

13. $^-5.2 \div 1.3$ _____

14. $5.13 \div {}^-0.3$ _____

15. $^-0.3 \cdot {}^-0.4 \cdot {}^-5.2$ _____

16. $\frac{1}{2} \cdot \left(16 \cdot \frac{-1}{15}\right)$ _____

Evaluate the expression for $l = {}^-0.5$ and $w = \frac{3}{5}$.

17. $^-15 \div w$ _____

18. $l \div 0.5$ _____

19. $w \cdot {}^-2.8$ _____

20. $15.5 \cdot w$ _____

21. $^-12.4 \cdot l$ _____

22. $w \div 0.2$ _____

23. $l \cdot 6.3$ _____

24. $l \cdot w$ _____

Find the value for n that makes each statement true.

25. $32 \div n = 4$ _____

26. $4 \cdot n = 1.6$ _____

27. $34 \div n = 17$ _____

Mixed Applications

28. The length of a stake that is dug into the ground deteriorates 0.12 inches every winter. If the stake is 15.5 inches long, how long will it be after 6 winters?

_____

29. The lake in Chris's back yard increases in volume by 1.12 liters every year. How long will it take for Chris's lake to increase by 30.24 liters?

_____

WRITER'S CORNER

30. Write a word problem similar to one of the Mixed Applications problems. Solve.

_____

_____

Solving One-Step Equations

Solve the equation. Check your solution.

1. $a + 4 = {}^-2$

2. $b - 2.5 = 2.5$

3. $0.25c = 4$

4. $d - 9.1 = 5.2$

5. $2.1e = 4.2$

6. $f + 3.4 = {}^-2.1$

7. $g + 0.1 = 1$

8. $-\frac{2}{3}h = 6$

9. $\frac{4}{7}j = 28$

10. $k - 1.2 = 3.1$

11. $m + 4 = 1.01$

12. $\frac{-n}{3} = 3$

Write an equation for the word sentence.

13. The sum of 1.3 and a number is 3.2.

14. A number decreased by 6.3 is $^-6.3$.

Mixed Applications

Write an equation for Exercise 15. Then solve.

15. There were $\frac{4}{5}$ as many cars at the race the second year than the first. If there were 32 cars the second year, how many cars were there the first?

16. It snowed 2.4 inches less this month than it did last month. If it snowed 10.3 inches this month, how much did it snow last month?

MIXED REVIEW

1. 12% of 300 is what number?_____

2. What percent of 2,700 is 405?_____

3. 48 is 60% of what number?_____

4. What is 18% of 240?_____

5. What is 9% of 32?_____

6. What percent of 85 is 34?_____

Solving Two-Step Equations

Solve the equation. Check your solution.

1. $2a + 5 = 1$

_____

2. $4b - 1 = 7$

_____

3. $0.5c - 12.25 = 2.25$

_____

4. $6f - 7 = {}^-10$

_____

5. $1.5h + 5 = 2$

_____

6. $6y + 8 = 14$

_____

7. ${}^-0.3j + 0.6 = 1.2$

_____

8. $11k + 7.7 = 15.4$

_____

9. $5w - {}^-2.5 = {}^-7.5$

_____

10. $\frac{m}{3} + 8 = {}^-7$

_____

11. $\frac{3}{7}n - 7 = 5$

_____

12. $\frac{7}{9}r + 3 = {}^-4$

_____

Write the calculator key sequence you can use to solve the equation.

13. $3y = 4(6 - 5)$

_____

14. $3(6 + 3) = 2z$

_____

15. $7(2.1 - 3) = 3f$

_____

Mixed Applications

Write an equation for Exercise 16. Then solve.

16. Jason scored 3 less than twice as many goals this week as he did last week. He scored 15 goals this week. How many goals did he score last week?

_____

17. Ms. Phipps made 12 dolls for gifts this year. She made $4\frac{1}{2}$ times that number last year. Find the total number of dolls she made this year and last year.

_____

LOGICAL REASONING

18. Which equation has a negative integer as its solution? _____

   a. $2n - 6 = {}^-12$ b. $14 - n = 6$

Solving Inequalities

Solve and graph the inequality.

1. $a + 5 < 4$

2. $b - 9 > 5$

3. $4c - 3 < 3$

_____

_____

_____

4. $\frac{4}{5}d \geq 8$

5. $e - 2 < 3$

6. $^-2f < 14$

_____

_____

_____

7. $^-4t \geq 3$

8. $^-5y < 10$

9. $^-3s + 2 < 8$

_____

_____

_____

Mixed Applications

Write an inequality for Exercise 10. Then solve.

10. At Mac's Sporting Goods, the number of bicycles sold in May was 40 less than the number sold in April. The total number sold in both months was less than the 120 bicycles sold in March. How many were sold in April and May?

11. Barbara rides her bicycle $2\frac{1}{3}$ mi each morning to deliver newspapers. How many miles does she ride in a week?

_____

_____   _____

MIXED REVIEW

Find the sum or difference.

1. $\frac{^-1}{4} - \frac{^-5}{8}$ _____

2. $^-3 + \frac{^-4}{7}$ _____

3. $\frac{^-4}{9} + \frac{7}{12}$ _____

4. $8 - {}^-4$ _____

5. $^-94 - 15$ _____

6. $19 + {}^-9$ _____

Problem-Solving Strategy
Use a Formula

Karen has poor night vision, and therefore drives her car $\frac{3}{5}$ as fast at night as she would during the day. In daylight, she averages 45 miles per hour on main roads and on side roads she averages 10 miles per hour.

Use this information to solve Exercises 1–2.

1. On Saturday Karen and her mother drove to her aunt's house, which is 108 miles away. Half of the distance was driven on the main road and half on side roads. If they drove there in daylight and came back at night, how much longer did the night trip take than the day trip?

2. One night Karen drove an hour on the main roads and 0.5 hours on the side roads. How far did she travel?

Mixed Applications ⟩	STRATEGIES	• Guess and Check • Use a Formula • Draw a Diagram • Work Backward

3. Carol spent $22.37 at the mall. If she spent $4.95 on a scarf, and $10.13 for a photo album, how much did she have left to spend?

4. Mike has a total of 212 marbles. He has three times as many white as he does black marbles. How many of each color does he have?

5. Bob's parents drove to his college in 3.5 hours. If Bob's dorm at college is 212 miles from home, how fast did his parents average in miles per hour?

6. Kevin and Smitty have 50 square feet of felt. They use the felt to cover a table that is 7 feet by 3.5 feet. How much felt do they have left over?

NUMBER SENSE

7. Two thirds of a number between 10 and 20, plus one half the number equals 2 more than the number. What is the number?

Graphing Ordered Pairs

Write the coordinates of the point.

1. B _____
2. H _____
3. A _____

4. I _____
5. D _____
6. F _____

7. C _____
8. E _____
9. L _____

10. G _____
11. J _____
12. O _____

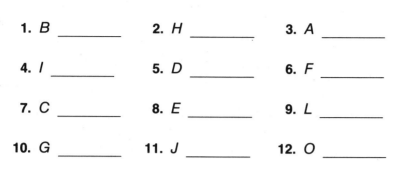

Name the point given by the coordinates.

13. (3,2) _____
14. (⁻2,5) _____
15. (6,⁻4) _____

16. (⁻1,⁻3) _____
17. (⁻5,3) _____
18. (7,0) _____

Draw a coordinate plane. Graph and label these points.

19. A(⁻4,2)
20. B(6,8)
21. C(⁻6,⁻2)

22. D(1,⁻4)
23. E(7,⁻3)
24. F(⁻1,8)

25. G($\frac{1}{2}$,4)
26. H(5,1$\frac{1}{2}$)

Mixed Applications

27. A bus drove 3 blocks south, 5 blocks east, 7 blocks north, and 10 blocks west. How many blocks south does the bus need to drive in order to be directly west of where it started? _____

28. Eighty bikers set out on a 20-mi ride. One fifth of the bikers stopped after 10 mi. One eighth of the remainder stopped after 13 mi. The rest finished the ride. What percent of the original group finished the ride? _____

VISUAL THINKING

29. A pilot has to land at Base 1, Base 2, and Base 3 on the map. Give the coordinates for each base.

_____

_____

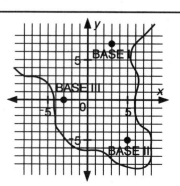

Relations and Functions

Write the ordered pairs for each relation. Write *yes* if the relation is a function and *no* if it is not.

1.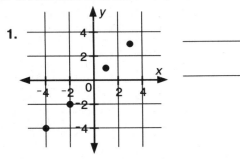

_____

_____

2.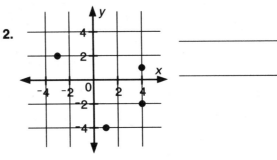

_____

_____

Write a word rule for each relation.

3.

Wages of Employees				
Hours, x	10	20	25	30
Wages, y	$100	$200	$250	$300

4.

Sale Prices				
Original price, x	$15	$20	$22	$28
Sale price, y	$10	$15	$17	$23

_____

_____

Mixed Applications

5. Kathy bought a new plant for her room. It will grow 4 in. every year. It is now 24 in. high. Make a table to show the relation between the height of the plant and the number of years for the next 5 years.

6. Michael spends 20% of his horseback riding time riding downhill. If he rode for 15 hr this week, how much time did he ride downhill?

_____

WRITER'S CORNER

7. The word rule for a relation is "divide the *x*-value by 2." Write a problem in which two items or situations show this relation.

_____

Equations with Two Variables

Make a table of values for each equation. Then write four ordered pairs that are solutions of each equation.

1. $y = x + 5$

_____

_____

2. $y = x - 3$

_____

_____

3. $y = 2x$

_____

_____

Determine whether the ordered pair is a solution of $y = 3x - 4$.
Write *yes* or *no.*

4. $(5,1)$ _____

5. $(^-2,2)$ _____

6. $(1,^-1)$ _____

7. $(\frac{1}{3},4)$ _____

Rewrite the equation to express y in terms of x. Then make a table of values for the equation. Let $x = ^-1, ^-\frac{1}{2}, 0, \frac{1}{2}$, and 1.

8. $x + y = 2$

_____

_____

9. $4x + y = 10$

_____

_____

10. $2x + 2y = 20$

_____

_____

Mixed Applications

11. The number of hours Julie practices her violin each week, *y,* is 3 hr more than the number of hours she studies, *x.* Write an equation to show the relationship of the two activities.

_____

12. Mark spends double the amount of time reading as he does listening to tapes. If he spends 4.5 hr reading and listening to tapes, how long does he spend doing each activity?

_____

EVERYDAY MATH CONNECTION

13. In order to find the number of kilometers in 30 mi, multiply the number of miles by 1.6 km. If x is the number of miles and y is the number of kilometers, this is the equation: $y = 1.6x$. There are 48 km in 30 mi, $48 = 1.6 \cdot 30$. Using the formula, how many kilometers are there in 40 mi?

_____

Graphing Equations

Use the graph of $y = x + 2$ for Exercises 1–4.

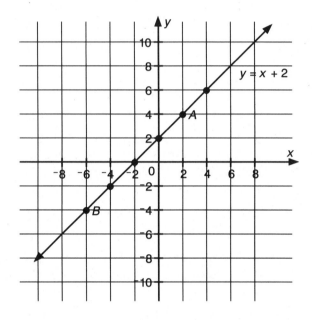

1. What is the solution of the equation

   at point A? _____

2. What is the solution of the equation

   at point B? _____

3. What is the value of x when the value

   of y is 2? _____

4. What is another solution of $y = x + 2$?

   _____

Graph the equations. Use at least three ordered pairs.

5. $y = x - 2$ 6. $y = 2x + 1$ 7. $y = x + 5$ 8. $y = 3x$

_____   _____   _____   _____

Mixed Applications

9. Stacey studies twice as long as Kathy. Write an equation to find the number of hours Stacey studies, y, when Kathy studies x hours. Graph the equation.

   _____

10. Use the graph in Exercise 9 to find how many hours Stacey studies when Kathy studies 4 hr.

    _____

LOGICAL REASONING

11. Since the graph of $y = x + 2$ is a straight line, how many solutions to the equation do you think there are?

    _____

94

Problem Solving
Use a Graph to Estimate

The graph shows the rate at which sound travels in air. Use the graph for Exercises 1–3.

1. About how many seconds does it take sound to travel 3 mi in air?

   _____

2. What is the approximate distance that sound travels in air in 4 sec?

   _____

3. Predict the approximate time it would take sound to travel 10 mi in air.

   _____

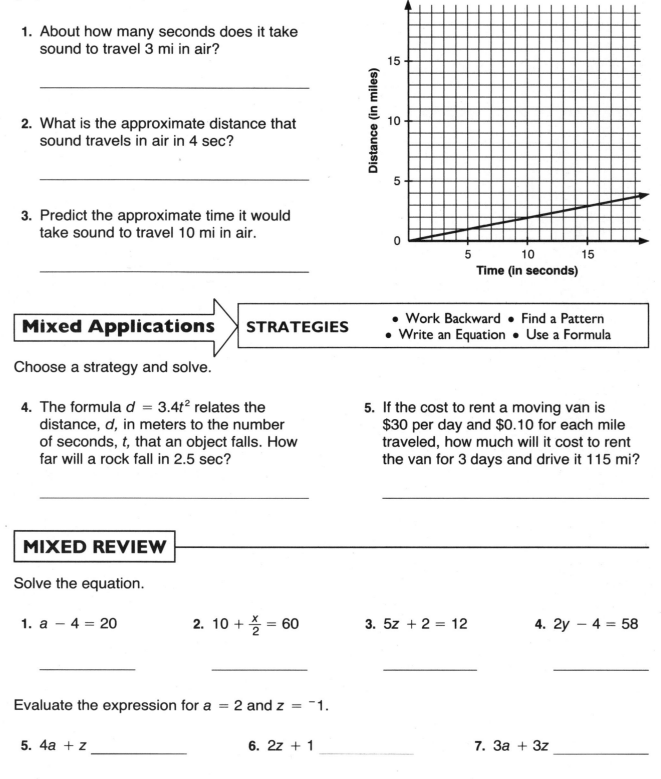

Distance (in miles)

Time (in seconds)

Mixed Applications > **STRATEGIES** | • Work Backward • Find a Pattern
• Write an Equation • Use a Formula

Choose a strategy and solve.

4. The formula $d = 3.4t^2$ relates the distance, d, in meters to the number of seconds, t, that an object falls. How far will a rock fall in 2.5 sec?

   _____

5. If the cost to rent a moving van is $30 per day and $0.10 for each mile traveled, how much will it cost to rent the van for 3 days and drive it 115 mi?

   _____

MIXED REVIEW

Solve the equation.

1. $a - 4 = 20$

2. $10 + \frac{x}{2} = 60$

3. $5z + 2 = 12$

4. $2y - 4 = 58$

_____   _____   _____   _____

Evaluate the expression for $a = 2$ and $z = {}^-1$.

5. $4a + z$ _____

6. $2z + 1$ _____

7. $3a + 3z$ _____

Exploring Slope of a Line

Find the slope of the line containing the given points.

1. (1,3), (2,4) _____

2. (3,6), (0,2) _____

3. (⁻1,2), (5,5) _____

4. (⁻1,⁻1), (⁻3,2) _____

5. (0,0), (6,⁻3) _____

6. (2,⁻5), (1,⁻2) _____

7. (4,⁻5), (⁻4,⁻5) _____

8. (0,5), (1,8) _____

9. (4,0), (⁻3,⁻2) _____

Write whether the slope is *positive* or *negative*.

10.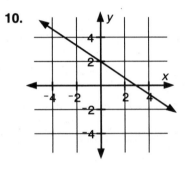

_____

11.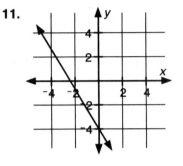

_____

12.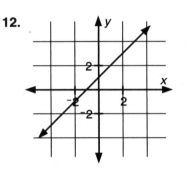

_____

13.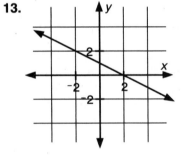

_____

14.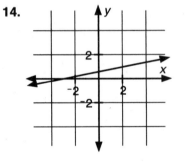

_____

15.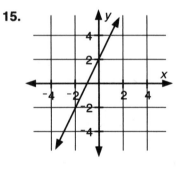

_____

SCIENCE CONNECTION

16. Find the slope of the line of the airplane landing, as shown.

_____

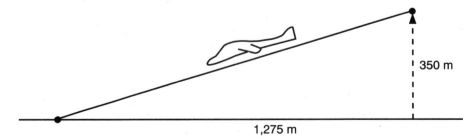

350 m

1,275 m

Exploring Systems of Equations

Solve the system by graphing.

1. $y = x - 2$

$y = {}^-x$ _____

2. $y = x + 4$

$y = 6 - x$ _____

3. $y = 2x - 2$

$y = 4x$ _____

Mixed Applications

Write a system of equations for each of Exercises 4–5. Solve the system by graphing.

4. John and Mark studied a total of 15 hr. Mark studied 3 more hours than John. How many hours did each study?

_____

_____

5. Jody exercised a total of 18 hr last week. She spent twice as much time jogging than doing sit-ups. How much time did she spend on each?

_____

_____

MIXED REVIEW

Compute.

1. $\frac{3}{2} + \frac{7}{2}$ _____

2. $\frac{3}{4} + \frac{5}{2}$ _____

3. $\frac{3}{10} + \frac{4}{5}$ _____

4. $\frac{4}{5} - \frac{2}{5}$ _____

5. $\frac{3}{9} - \frac{5}{3}$ _____

6. $\frac{32}{21} - \frac{5}{7}$ _____

7. $\frac{6}{9} \times \frac{1}{3}$ _____

8. $\frac{7}{2} \times \frac{10}{3}$ _____

9. $\frac{20}{13} \times \frac{11}{2}$ _____

10. $\frac{4}{9} \div \frac{5}{12}$ _____

11. $\frac{6}{11} \div \frac{7}{2}$ _____

12. $\frac{1}{9} \div \frac{3}{8}$ _____

Exploring Graphs of Inequalities

Graph each inequality.

1. $y > x - 2$

2. $y < 3 - x$

3. $y \leq 2x$

Use the graph of $y > x + 5$ for Exercises 4–6.

4. Name an ordered pair that is a solution of the inequality.

_____

5. Is (3,5) a solution of $y > x + 5$?

_____

6. Name an ordered pair that is a solution of $y \leq x + 5$.

_____

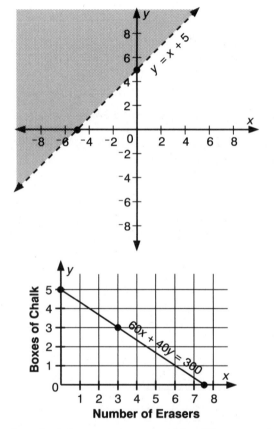

Mixed Applications

A box of chalk costs $0.60. One eraser is $0.40. Use the graph for Exercises 7 and 8. In the graph, (2,3) means a purchase of 2 erasers and 3 boxes of chalk.

7. Ms. Wo can spend up to $3.00 for chalk and erasers. If she buys no erasers, how many boxes of chalk can she buy?

_____

8. In what three ways can Ms. Wo spend exactly $3.00? Write the answers as ordered pairs.

_____

LOGICAL REASONING

9. Find a four-digit number such that the product of the middle two digits is 35 and the product of the first and fourth digits is 21. The third and fourth digits are less than the first and second digits. _____

Transformations

Give the coordinates of the point that is a translation of the given point.

1. Move (3,6) 4 units down. _____

2. Move (5,8) 6 units left. _____

3. Move (‾1,2) 2 units up

and 4 units right. _____

4. Move (‾3,‾4) 2 units down

and 6 units right. _____

Using the *x*-axis as the line of symmetry, give the coordinates of the point that is the reflection of the given point.

5. (5,2) _____

6. (2,0) _____

7. (‾4,5) _____

Using the *y*-axis as the line of symmetry, give the coordinates of the point that is the reflection of the given point.

8. (4,1) _____

9. (‾3,5) _____

10. (‾2,‾8) _____

Copy quadrilateral *ABCD* on a coordinate plane. Then draw the rotation. Use (0,0) as the point of rotation.

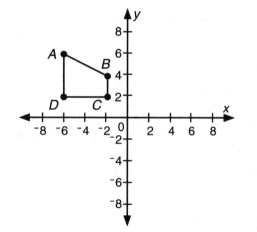

11. Rotate 90° clockwise.

12. Rotate 180° clockwise.

13. Rotate 270° counterclockwise.

Mixed Applications

14. Quadrilateral *ABCD* has vertices *A*(‾5,5),*B*(‾5,0),*C*(‾1,2), and *D*(‾1,4). Rotate the quadrilateral 180° counterclockwise. What are the coordinates of the quadrilateral if the rotation point is (0,‾1)?

_____

15. A train and a bus each leave at 10:00 A.M. from towns 45 mi apart. They travel toward each other. The bus travels at 40 mph. The train travels at 50 mph. At what time do they meet?

_____

ART CONNECTION

16. Draw a figure on a coordinate plane. Rotate your figure both 90° counterclockwise and 90° clockwise.

Problem-Solving Strategy
Guess and Check

1. Tickets for the school play cost $6.00 for adults and $3.50 for students. Mark paid $13.00 for fewer than 3 tickets of each type. How many adult tickets and how many student tickets did Mark buy?

   _____

2. Judy sold some records for $1.00 each and some tapes for $1.50 each. She sold fewer than 5 of each type and collected $8.50 in all. How many of each did she sell?

   _____

3. Andy delivers the local paper at $0.55 each and the city paper at $1.10 each. He delivered fewer than 5 papers of each type and collected $4.40. How many of each type did he deliver?

   _____

4. Joan bought some pencils for $0.15 each and some pens for $0.35 each. She has fewer than 7 in all. How many pens and how many pencils did she buy for $1.50?

   _____

Mixed Applications >	STRATEGIES	• Draw a Diagram • Guess and Check • Make a Table • Write an Equation

Choose a strategy and solve.

5. The school newspaper club published 20,000 newspapers. On Monday, the club sold 50% of the newspapers. Each day thereafter, the club sold 20% of the remaining newspapers. How many newspapers were left to sell after Friday?

   _____

6. At a soccer game, the students sold hot dogs for $1.00 each and soda for $0.75 a can. How many hot dogs and how many cans of soda did they sell if they made $16.75? Give all possible combinations.

   _____

   _____

   _____

LOGICAL REASONING

7. The local theater seats 102 people. At the play on Friday night, there was one empty seat for every two occupied seats. How many people were at the play?

   _____

Analyzing Data: Mean, Median, and Mode

Find the mean, median, and mode for each set of data. Round the answers for Exercises 1–4 to the nearest hundredth.

1. 70, 72, 75, 75, 78, 80, 80

_____

2. 2.63, 9.61, 3.057, 8.39, 5.12

_____

3. 3 lbs, 7 lbs, 5 lbs

_____

4. 20, 25, 25, 35, 40

_____

Use the data in Exercise 1. Write the number or numbers that you can remove from the set of data to make each statement correct.

5. There is no mode _____

6. The mode is 80 _____

Write *true* or *false* for each.

7. Some sets of data do not have a mean.

8. There is always a mode for each set of data.

_____

_____

Mixed Applications

Tim worked in a store during the summer. The hours he worked one week were 2, 3, 3, 4, 3, 5, 1.

9. Find the mean, median, and mode for the data.

_____

10. What was the total number of hours he worked during the week?

_____

WRITER'S CORNER

11. Write a problem using the data for Exercises 9-10. Solve.

_____

_____

Frequency Tables and Histograms

1. Make a side-by-side frequency table and a side-by-side histogram for the geography test scores.

Geography Test Scores					
Boys			Girls		
25	32	26	27	35	39
40	39	28	28	24	21

Boys		Girls		
Tally	Frequency	Score	Frequency	Tally
		36–40		
		31–35		
		26–30		
		21–25		

Geography Test Scores					
Boys		Scores	Girls		
		36–40			
		31–35			
		26–30			
		21–25			

2. What is the range of scores for both girls and boys?_____

3. How many students have scores in the interval 36–40?_____

Mixed Applications

Use the histogram to answer Exercises 4 and 5.

4. Did more men or women use the library on Monday evening?

   _____

Monday Evening Library Users		
Men	Ages	Women
	51 and over	
	41–50	
	31–40	
	21–30	
	11–20	
12 10 8 6 4 2		2 4 6 8 10

5. How many people under 21 years of age used the library on Monday evening? _____

SOCIAL STUDIES CONNECTION

6. Find a graph. Decide whether the data in that graph could have been presented in a histogram. Explain.

_____

Line Graphs

1. Circle the graph that represents this situation. You are driving at 25 miles per hour. After some time you increase speed to the speed limit and maintain that speed. Then you slow down to 25 miles per hour.

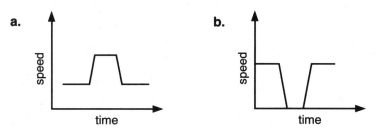

a.

b.

c.

2. Construct a double-line graph for the data in the following table.

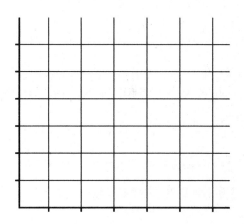

Average Monthly Precipitation (in inches)						
	Jan.	Feb.	March	April	May	June
Morgantown	0.7	0.8	0.7	0.6	1.0	1.1
Lowell	3.2	2.7	1.6	0.5	0.5	0.5

Mixed Applications

Use the data and your line graph to answer Exercises 3 and 4.

3. What is the total rainfall for January through June for Morgantown?

_____

4. Which town has a more consistent amount of rainfall?

_____

WRITER'S CORNER

5. Describe a school-related situation for which a double-line graph would be a good way to present the data.

_____

_____

_____

Problem Solving
Sufficient and Insufficient Data

The table shows the minimum and maximum temperatures of the major cities in the Northeast. Also, weather warnings, if any, are given in the table. Use this table for Exercises 1–4. Write *sufficient* or *insufficient* for each question. Then answer those questions for which the data is sufficient.

1. Is there a snow forecast for New York?

   _____

2. When will it rain in Boston?

   _____

Weather Forecast for Nov. 12–17			
City	Minimum Temp.	Maximum Temp.	Warnings
New York	34°F	45°F	snow
Pittsburgh	30°F	50°F	– – – –
Boston	32°F	47°F	windy
Princeton	31°F	44°F	rain

3. What will the average temperature in Pittsburgh be for November 12–17?

   _____

4. What range of temperatures is shown for Princeton?

   _____

Mixed Applications ⟩ STRATEGIES	• Guess and Check • Work Backward • Find a Pattern • Use a Formula

Choose a strategy and solve.

5. Five students took an aptitude test. Their scores were 50, 70, 60, 65, and 55. What is the average score?

   _____

6. Johnson Associates buy shirts for $24 per dozen. They sell each shirt at $3. What is the profit per dozen?

   _____

MIXED REVIEW

Row-Along Canoe Rental Monthly Rental Income (in dollars)					
May	June	July	Aug.	Sept.	Oct.
$2,500	$5,050	$8,900	$8,750	$4,200	$1,800

For the monthly rental income, find the

1. mean _____

2. median _____

3. mode _____

Bar Graphs

1. Construct a double-bar graph that compares average monthly precipitation for January and July.

Average Monthly Precipitation (in inches)		
City	Jan.	July
Albany, NY	2.4	3.0
Chicago, IL	1.6	3.6
Omaha, NE	0.8	3.6
Norfolk, VA	3.7	5.2

Use your graph for Exercises 2–5.

2. Which city has the greatest amount of precipitation during the month of January?

_____

3. Which city has an average precipitation for both January and July of greater than 3 inches?

_____

4. Which city has the least precipitation during the month of July?

_____

5. What is the range of precipitation shown in the graph?

_____

Mixed Applications

Use your bar graph for Exercise 6.

6. Rebecca lives in Albany, NY. Which city should she move to if she wants the amount of precipitation to be about the same as Albany?

_____

7. Mr. Gomez drove from Albany to Chicago in about 16 hours. His average speed was 53 miles per hour. How many miles did he drive?

_____

SOCIAL STUDIES CONNECTION

8. What is the average precipitation in your area during the months of January and July? How does it compare with that of the cities in the bar graph?

_____

_____

Circle Graphs

Use the Shywood Eagles baseball data for Exercises 1–8.

Shywood Eagles Baseball (number of games)		
Won	Lost	Tied
7	5	2

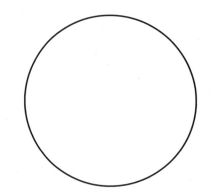

1. How many games did the Eagles play?

_____   _____

Find the percent of the total number of games represented by each.

2. games won _____

3. games lost _____

4. games tied _____

Find the central angle measure to represent each. Round to the nearest degree.

5. games won _____

6. games lost _____

7. games tied _____

8. Use the circle above to construct a circle graph to represent the Shywood Eagle's baseball record. Give your graph a title.

Mixed Applications

Use the circle graph in Exercise 8 for Exercises 9–10.

9. What does the graph show about Ties and Losses together as a percent of the total?

_____

_____

10. If the Eagles had played and won 7 more games, what percent of the total number would they have won?

_____

NUMBER SENSE

11. If 5% of the central angle measure of a circle equals 18°,

75% equals _____ .

Making Inferences

Display the Cook Corporation data in a line graph. Then use the
table and graph for Exercises 1–3.

Cook Corporation Revenue			
Year	Revenue (in millions)	Year	Revenue (in millions)
1800	$6.2	1900	$75
1820	$8.9	1920	$107
1840	$16	1940	$133
1860	$30	1960	$180
1880	$50	1980	$230

1. What is the trend for the data?

   _____

2. What is the interpolation of the revenue
   received in 1870?

   _____

3. Predict the revenue for the year 2000. _____

Mixed Applications

Use the Cook Corporation Revenue table and graph for
Exercises 4–6.

4. What is the increase in the revenue
   between 1900 and 1960?

   _____

5. What might the revenue have been for 1970?

   _____

6. What is the average revenue for the
   years given?

   _____

SOCIAL STUDIES CONNECTION

7. Use an encyclopedia or other reference book to research some
   of the different types of statistics that the U.S. government
   keeps on population. List some of these statistics and tell how
   you think they are used.

   _____

   _____

Fundamental Counting Principle

Find the total number of choices.

1. ties: red, blue, green
shirts: white, pink

_____

2. drink: apple juice
sandwich: hamburger, grilled cheese

_____

3. picnics: national park, zoo
dates: March, April

_____

4. pattern: stripes, round, plain
size: small, medium, large

_____

Mr. Ames is going to buy a new TV. The table shows his choices. Use the table for Exercises 5–7.

Types	Sizes	Options
Color	13 in.	Stereo
Black & White	20 in.	Remote control
	24 in.	Picture in picture

5. How many total choices does Mr. Ames have to choose from?

_____

6. If Mr. Ames does not want any options, how many choices does he have?

_____

7. If Mr. Ames wants a 20-in. color TV, how many options does he have?

_____

Mixed Applications

8. A restaurant has 5 appetizers, 10 entrees and 6 salads. In how many different ways can a person order a meal that includes an entree, an appetizer, and a salad?

_____

9. If 20 eggs cost $2.00, what is the cost of a dozen eggs?

_____

WRITER'S CORNER

10. Write a problem involving choices and shopping. Exchange problems with a friend. Solve.

_____

_____

Permutations

Find the value. You may use a calculator.

1. $4!$ **2.** $\frac{8!}{3!}$ **3.** $\frac{12!}{(12-8)!}$ **4.** $4! - 3!$ **5.** $2! + 4!$

_____   _____   _____   _____   _____

Write the number of permutations as a factorial expression.

6. $_5P_3$ **7.** $_5P_5$ **8.** $_7P_5$ **9.** $_{20}P_3$ **10.** $_4P_3$

_____   _____   _____   _____   _____

Find the number of permutations. You may use a calculator.

11. $_{20}P_2$ **12.** $_{15}P_3$ **13.** $_7P_7$ **14.** $_8P_4$ **15.** $_{11}P_6$

_____   _____   _____   _____   _____

16. Complete the table.

Kind of Number	Digits Used	Number of Permutations (without repeating digits)
two-digit	2, 4, 6, 8	_____
three-digit	1, 3, 6, 8, 9, 4	_____
four-digit	1, 4, 6, 8, 9, 7	_____
five-digit	1, 2, 3, 4, 5, 6, 7, 8, 9	_____

Mixed Applications

17. In how many ways can a quarterback and receiver be chosen from 9 players?

18. Of the 18 students in the hiking club, $\frac{1}{2}$ of them are inexperienced, and $\frac{1}{3}$ of them are very experienced. How many are in between?

GEOGRAPHY CONNECTION

19. A tour guide offers tours to these countries in Central America: Belize, Guatemala, Nicaragua, Costa Rica, El Salvador, Honduras, and Panama. In how many ways can a tour guide arrange tours of 2 countries?

_____

Probability

You spin the spinner. Find each probability.

1. P(2) _____

2. P(not 4) _____

3. P(3 or 2) _____

4. P(1, 4, or 5) _____

5. P(5 and white) _____

6. P(5 or white) _____

You roll a number cube numbered from 1 to 6. Find each probability.

7. P(5) _____

8. P(3 or 4) _____

9. P(not 5) _____

10. P(number > 3) _____

11. P(odd number) _____

12. P(number < 1) _____

13. What is the sample space when you flip three coins?

_____

Mixed Applications

14. If you throw a cube numbered 1–6, an even number gets you a prize. What is the probability that you will win a prize on a throw?

_____

15. Free science catalogs are being distributed. They have blue, green, red, or orange covers. What is the probability that the catalog you receive will have a green cover?

_____

MIXED REVIEW

Write the fraction in the simplest form.

1. $\frac{12}{15}$ _____

2. $\frac{24}{15}$ _____

3. $\frac{35}{50}$ _____

4. $\frac{18}{81}$ _____

Compute.

5. $\frac{4 \times 2}{3 \times 2} =$ _____

6. $\frac{5 \times 6 \times 7}{1 \times 2 \times 3} =$ _____

7. $\frac{12 \times 10 \times 9}{60} =$ _____

Exploring Pascal's Triangle

1. Complete Pascal's Triangle.

Row 0   1

Row 1   1   1

Row 2   1   ___   1

Row 3   1   ___   ___   1

Row 4   1   ___   ___   ___   1

You toss 4 coins. Find the probability. Use the numbers and their sum from Row 4 of Pascal's Triangle.

2. P(4 heads) _____   3. P(4 tails) _____   4. P(3 tails) _____

You toss 5 coins. Find the probability.

5. P(5 heads) _____   6. P(4 tails) _____   7. P(4 heads) _____

Use Pascal's Triangle for Exercises 8–9.

8. Complete Row 5 and give its elements.   9. Complete Row 6 and give its elements.

_____   _____

Use Pascal's Triangle.

10. Find the sum of the numbers in Rows 0–5.   11. Give the second element in Row 8.

_____   _____

WRITER'S CORNER

12. Explain how to find the numbers for a row of Pascal's Triangle using the numbers in the row above.

_____

_____

Problem Solving
Use a Diagram

Use Pascal's Triangle to solve.

1. A yacht club with 10 members wants to elect 4 officers. How many combinations of 4 officers can be elected from the 10 members?

_____

2. Two students in an eighth grade class with 12 students will win an award. In how many ways can 2 winners be chosen from 12 students?

_____

3. There are 9 members of the art club, but only 3 of them may go to an art exhibition. In how many ways can the three persons be selected?

_____

4. The bicycle shop has 10 models of bicycles. Of these, 6 will be displayed in the window. In how many ways can the selection be made?

_____

Mixed Applications

STRATEGIES	• Draw a Diagram • Find a Pattern • Use a Formula • Work Backward

Choose a strategy and solve.

5. Noel is arranging 10 books on a shelf. In how many ways can the books be placed?

_____

6. Mara earned $3,000. If she repaid a loan of $500 with 10% interest, how much money did she have left?

_____

7. Tai drove 200 miles in $3\frac{1}{2}$ hours. What was his average speed?

_____

8. A bus traveled for $2\frac{2}{3}$ hr at a speed of 55 mph. How far did the bus travel?

_____

MIXED REVIEW

Solve for x.

1. $x + 3 = \frac{210}{7}$

_____

2. $5x - 10 = \frac{80}{2}$

_____

3. $4.5x = 68.4$

_____

4. Circle the ratio that is equivalent to 4 to 7.

   a. 1 to 5   b. 16 to 28   c. 7 to 4   d. 14 to 21

Random Numbers

The random numbers 0–9 in the table were generated by a computer. Use the table for Exercises 1–4.

50 random numbers

1	2	4	5	8	7	3	5	7	9
3	5	7	2	6	9	4	7	2	0
2	6	0	7	4	2	7	8	3	8
2	6	5	4	8	0	9	2	5	6
2	8	7	4	5	0	8	9	2	5

1. You are playing a game using the spinner shown. Use the table to simulate 50 spins. How many spins will it take before you get all the numbers from 0–9?

_____

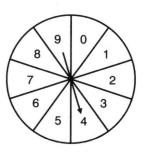

2. Use the spinner again with the table. How many spins will it take to get number 7 twice?

_____

3. Using the mathematical probability, predict how many times the spinner will stop on 5 if you spin 40 times.

_____

4. What is the probability of getting number 3 in 10 spins? Use the data from the table.

_____

Mixed Applications

5. Jean put 10 cards numbered 0–9 in a bag. Amy takes a card out and puts it back. Predict the number of times Susan will pick the 2-card if she picks 50 times. How does your prediction compare with the results of the table?

_____

6. José went to buy car tires. Each tire cost him $30. If he wanted to change all of his 4 tires, how much would it cost him?

_____

WRITER'S CORNER

7. Computer programmers often use random numbers in writing many different kinds of programs. Describe two kinds of programs in which random numbers might be useful.

_____

_____

_____

Predictions

Frank tosses a baseball card into the air. The card lands face up
30 out of 50 times. Use this information for Exercises 1–4.

1. What is the experimental probability that the card will land face up on the next toss?

   _____

2. What is the experimental probability that the card will land facedown on the next toss?

   _____

3. How many times can you expect the card to land face up in the next 75 tosses?

   _____

4. How many times can you expect the card to land facedown in the next 25 tosses?

   _____

Alison is on the basketball team. She has made 7 out of 10 free
throws. Use this information for Exercises 5–6.

5. What is the experimental probability that she will make her next free throw?

   _____

6. How many of the next 20 free throws can she expect to miss?

   _____

Mixed Applications

The table shows the TV show preferences of 500 students.
Use the table for Exercises 7–10.

7. What is the experimental probability that a seventh grader will prefer comedy?

   _____

8. What is the experimental probability that a sixth grader will prefer news?

   _____

TV Show Preferences			
	Comedy	News	Cartoons
Sixth Graders	20	26	34
Seventh Graders	30	46	44
Eighth Graders	44	46	30

9. Of 280 eighth graders, how many could be expected to prefer comedy?

   _____

10. What percent of the seventh graders prefer news?

    _____

Independent Events

Two nickels are tossed and a number cube is rolled. Find the probability.

1. P(two heads, 4)

_____

2. p(one tail, odd number)

_____

3. p(2 tails, even number)

_____

4. p(two heads, not 3)

_____

5. p(not tails, 7)

_____

6. p(1 tail, 2 or 4)

_____

You spin the spinners. Find the probability.

7. p(blue, 2)

_____

8. p(red, 6)

_____

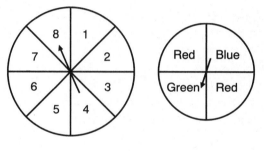

9. p(not blue, odd number)

_____

10. p(red, not 8)

_____

11. p(red, 5, red)

_____

12. p(not red, 8)

_____

Mixed Applications

13. Sheila throws two coins at a time. She will win the game if she gets two like events. What is the probability she will win?

_____

14. Joe correctly answered 70% of the questions on a test. There were 50 questions. How many questions did Joe answer correctly?

_____

MIXED REVIEW

Find the product.

1. $\frac{1}{2} \times \frac{1}{4}$ _____

2. $\frac{2}{3} \times \frac{1}{5}$ _____

3. $\frac{34}{4} \times \frac{1}{3}$ _____

4. Find the mean, median and mode of 73, 64, 92, 73, 83, 79, 96

_____

Dependent Events

A jar contains these balls—2 green, 3 white, and 5 black. Select one ball at random. Without replacing it, select a second ball. Find the probabilities.

1. P(white, then green)

_____

2. P(green, then black)

_____

3. P(black, then black)

_____

Without replacing a ball, select a third ball. Find the probabilities.

4. P(black, then black, then black)

_____

5. P(white, then white, then green)

_____

6. P(white, then green, then green)

_____

7. P(black, then green, then white)

_____

A box contains 5 red marbles, 3 blue marbles, and 7 white marbles. The marbles are selected at random, one at a time, and not replaced. Find the probabilities.

8. P(red, then blue)

_____

9. P(red, then white)

_____

10. P(red, then white, then blue)

_____

11. P(white, then white, then white)

_____

Mixed Applications

12. Janette picks from a deck of 52 playing cards. What is the probability that she will pick a king?

_____

13. In Exercise 12, if Janette picks up a second card without replacing the first one, what is the probability that she will pick a king again?

_____

WRITER'S CORNER

14. Throw a cube numbered 1–6 25 times. Write the outcome of each throw. Write a probability question based on your outcomes. Solve.

Venn Diagrams

Draw Venn diagrams for these statements.

1. Some students play both soccer and football.

2. Some multiples of 5 are odd numbers.

Use the Venn diagram for Exercises 3–6.

3. How many students are there in total?

   _____

4. How many play football but not rugby?

   _____

5. How many play rugby but not football? _____

6. How many play rugby and football? _____

FOOTBALL   RUGBY

30   7   20

Mixed Applications

7. In a fine arts club of 20 members, 10 members are only painters and 3 members are both painters and dancers. How many members are only dancers?

   _____

8. Draw a Venn diagram that shows the relationships in Exercise 7.

SOCIAL STUDIES CONNECTION

9. There are 11 buildings in Cincinnati, Ohio, that are over 300 feet tall. Five of these buildings have more than 30 stories. One building has exactly 30 stories. Make a Venn diagram showing these facts.

Precision: Greatest Possible Error

Give the precision of each measurement.

1. 9 m

2. $4\frac{1}{4}$ ft

3. $7\frac{1}{8}$ in.

4. 3.5 km

_____   _____   _____   _____

Find the greatest possible error of each measurement.

5. 65 mm

6. 23 yd

7. 7.5 m

8. 7.85 km

_____   _____   _____   _____

9. $170\frac{1}{4}$ ft

10. $3\frac{1}{3}$ mi.

11. 0.354 m

12. $23\frac{3}{16}$ ft

_____   _____   _____   _____

For the given measurement, tell how small and how large the actual measure can be.

13. 50 mi.

14. 60 mm

15. 34.5 km

16. $11\frac{1}{2}$ yd

_____   _____   _____   _____

Mixed Applications

17. A shark was found to be 6 feet long. What is the greatest possible error of this measurement?

18. The swimming pool in the gym is 12 ft deep. Find the largest and smallest value for the actual depth.

_____   _____

19. There are more than 15,000 kinds of books in the library. The smallest are science manuals with a width of 14 cm. The largest are atlases with a width of 36 cm. Write a question using this information.

_____

_____

_____

Exploring Significant Digits

Find the appropriate number of significant digits for each answer.

1. 1 m + 3.2 m

_____

2. 12.3 m − 10.34 m

_____

3. 2.1 m × 1.38 m

_____

Find each sum or difference. Use rounding to express the answer with the correct number of significant digits.

4. 16.87 m + 13 m

_____

5. 20.324 m − 10.1 m

_____

6. 3.28 m + 7.354 m

_____

Find each product. Use rounding to express the answer with the correct number of significant digits.

7. 2.3 m × 2 m

_____

8. 3.84 m × 2 m

_____

9. 3.50 m × 1.1 m

_____

Mixed Applications

10. A boat can carry a load of 1,000 lb (to the nearest pound). How many significant digits does this measure have?

_____

11. A building is 100 ft tall (to the nearest foot). How many significant digits does this height have?

_____

MIXED REVIEW

Write the reciprocal.

1. 4

_____

2. $\frac{1}{7}$

_____

3. $\frac{3}{5}$

_____

4. $\frac{6}{8}$

_____

Find the sum or difference.

5. 1.2 + 3.4

_____

6. 3.45 − 1.45

_____

7. 1.234 + 3.450

_____

Problem-Solving Strategy
Make a Model

An art gallery is creating paper cuttings in a variety of geometric shapes. Find the required number of paper cuttings for each of the four exhibits.

1. How many 4-in. square cuttings are required for an 8 in. by 8 in. rectangular exhibit?

   _____

2. How many 1-in. square cuttings are required for a 12 in. by 12 in. square exhibit?

   _____

3. How many 2-in. equilateral triangle cuttings are required for a regular hexagon whose sides each measure 2 in.?

   _____

4. How many 2 in. equilateral triangle cuttings are required to complete an equilateral triangle whose sides each measure 8 in.?

   _____

| **Mixed Applications** > | **STRATEGIES** | • Make a Model • Write an Equation • Solve a Simpler Problem • Work Backward |

Choose a strategy and solve.

5. Liang uses 5 cups of orange juice in his punch to serve 10 people. How many cups of orange juice should he use to serve 95 people?

   _____

6. A steel rod is sold in 5-ft sections at $10 a section. What is the cost for fencing a straight 110-ft fence?

   _____

7. Carmen went on a business trip. She traveled by car. Her employer paid 25¢ for each mile, for a total of $675. How many miles did she travel?

   _____

8. Garnetta now weighs 98 pounds. Last week she lost 3 pounds. The week before she gained 2 pounds. How much did she weigh 2 weeks ago?

   _____

ART CONNECTION

9. Make a scale drawing for the floor plan of a building you design. Label the length and width of each room with the correct measurement, depending upon the scale you choose.

Perimeter of Polygons

Find the perimeter.

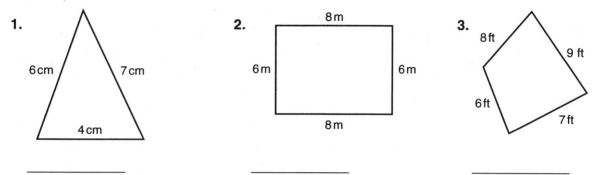

1. 6 cm 7 cm 4 cm

_____

2. 8 m 6 m 6 m 8 m

_____

3. 8 ft 9 ft 6 ft 7 ft

_____

Find the perimeter of each regular polygon.

4. 10 in.

_____

5. 2 m

_____

6. 3 ft

_____

The perimeter of each polygon is given. Find the missing length.

7. $P = 43.5$ cm

_____

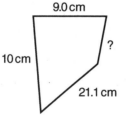

9.0 cm 10 cm ? 21.1 cm

8. $P = 90$ in.

_____

? 38 in. 40 in.

Mixed Applications

9. Is 900 ft of fencing enough to enclose a garden 350 ft long by 150 ft wide?

_____

10. Enola uses 400 ft of fencing to enclose her garden, a 90-ft wide rectangle. What is the length of the garden?

_____

| **WRITER'S CORNER** |

11. Write a question involving the perimeter of a triangle. Solve.

_____

Circumference of Circles

Find the circumference to the nearest hundredth. Use 3.14 for π.

1. $r = 4.055$ cm

2. $r = 0.03$ cm

3. $d = 0.48$ m

4. $d = 0.92$ km

_____ _____ _____ _____

Find the circumference. Use $\frac{22}{7}$ for π.

5. $r = 7$ in.

6. $r = 21$ yd

7. $d = 56$ ft

8. $r = 35$ ft

_____ _____ _____ _____

Find the diameter of each circle. The circumference is given. Use 3.14 for π.

9. 131.88 ft

10. 1.57 m

11. 314 in.

_____ _____ _____

12. Which is greater, the perimeter of the square or the circumference of the circle?

_____

12 m (square)   12 m (circle diameter)

Mixed Applications

13. A tree is surrounded with a circular retaining wall 3 m in diameter. What is the circumference of the retaining wall?

_____

14. A circular fountain is surrounded by a fence. If the radius of the fountain is 5 ft, what is the amount of fencing needed?

_____

MIXED REVIEW

Find the perimeter for the following squares. The length of a side is given.

1. 5 cm

2. 20 m

3. 4 km

4. 6 cm

5. 7 yd

_____ _____ _____ _____ _____

Find the product.

6. $^-7 \times {}^-3 =$ _____

7. $18 \times {}^-3 =$ _____

8. $2 \times {}^-14 \cdot {}^-2 =$ _____

Area of Rectangles and Parallelograms

Find the area of each polygon.

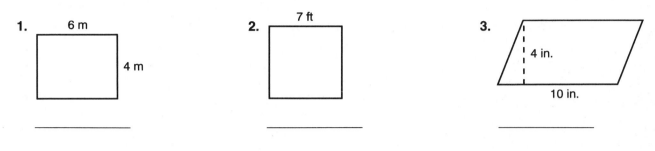

1. 6 m 4 m

_____

2. 7 ft

_____

3. 4 in. 10 in.

_____

Find the area of each rectangle.

4. l = 6 in., w = 3 in.

_____

5. l = 12 m, w = 8 m

_____

6. l = 9.4 m, w = 6.7 m

_____

Find the area of the shaded region of each figure.

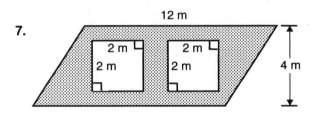

7. 12 m 2 m 2 m 2 m 2 m 4 m

_____

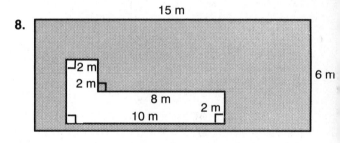

8. 15 m 2 m 2 m 8 m 2 m 10 m 6 m

_____

Mixed Applications

9. A rectangular pan is 10 in. wide and has a length of 14 in. What is the area of the pan?

_____

10. Mr. Santiago bought a rug with an area of 2,500 sq. in. Will the rug fit in the front hall, which is 48 in. by 60 in.?

_____

_____

┌─────────────────────────────────────┐
│ **SOCIAL STUDIES CONNECTION** │
└─────────────────────────────────────┘

11. The state of Wyoming is roughly rectangular in shape. It has an area of more than 96,000 square miles. Write some possible dimensions of the state's length and width.

_____

Area of Triangles and Trapezoids

Find the area of each triangle.

1. $b = 4$ cm, $h = 6$ cm

2. $b = 10$ ft, $h = 5$ ft

_____

_____

Find the area of each trapezoid.

3. $h = 6$ cm, $b_1 = 2$ cm, $b_2 = 4$ cm

4. $h = 9$ m, $b_1 = 10$ m, $b_2 = 2$ m

_____

_____

Find the area of each shaded region.

5.

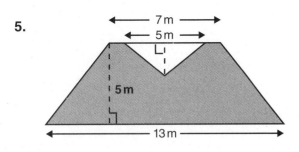

6.

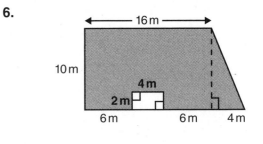

_____

_____

Mixed Applications

7. The front wall of a building is trapezoidal in shape. Its bases are 12 m and 14 m. The height of the building is 10 m. What is the area of the front wall?

_____

8. The rectangular base of a computer is 1 ft by 2 ft. The area of the base of the monitor is 4 ft^2. What is the total area occupied by both the base of the computer and the monitor?

_____

ART CONNECTION

9. Make a design composed of triangles and trapezoids. Make the measure of each side of each figure a whole number. Calculate the area of the entire drawing.

Area Of Circles

Find the area to the nearest hundredth. Use 3.14 for π.

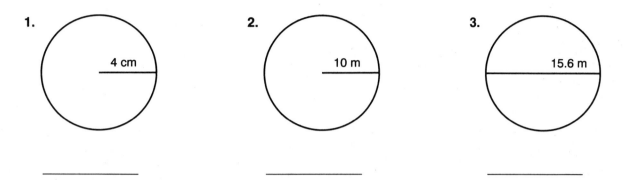

1. 4 cm

_____

2. 10 m

_____

3. 15.6 m

_____

Find the area of the shaded region.

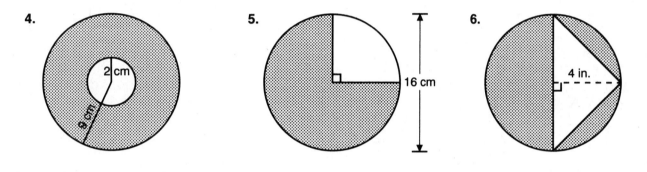

4. 2 cm / 8 cm

_____

5. 16 cm

_____

6. 4 in.

_____

Mixed Applications

7. A satellite antenna is circular in shape. If the diameter is 10 m, what is the area of the antenna?

_____

8. A certain clock has a circular face. If the area of the face is 113.04 in.^{2}, what is its circumference?

_____

MIXED REVIEW

Evaluate the expression for $n = 10$.

1. $8n$

_____

2. $n + 12$

_____

3. $\frac{n}{2}$

_____

4. $2n + 1$

_____

Write a decimal for the fraction.

5. $\frac{3}{20}$ _____

6. $\frac{4}{25}$ _____

7. $\frac{3}{50}$ _____

8. $\frac{14}{28}$ _____

125

Problem-Solving Strategy
Use a Formula

Use the formula $R = \frac{Ph}{3} - w$ for Exercises 1–4.

    R = number of rolls of paper
    P = perimeter of room (in meters)
    h = height of room (in meters)
    w = reduction for doors and windows (1 roll for every door
        and 1 roll for every 2 windows)

1. An office is 2 m wide and 3 m long with a 3-m ceiling. There are 2 windows and 1 door. How many rolls of wallpaper are needed?

2. A store is 10 m wide and 20 m long with a 5-m ceiling. There are 5 doors and 10 windows. How many rolls of wallpaper are needed?

3. A dining room is 3 m wide and 4 m long with a 3-m ceiling. There are 2 windows and 1 door. If wallpaper costs $10 a roll, what will be the total cost?

4. A bedroom in a hotel measures 4 m wide and 5 m long with a 2.5-m ceiling. There are 4 windows and 2 doors. How many rolls of wallpaper are needed?

Mixed Applications ⟩ **STRATEGIES**
    • Use a Formula • Draw a Diagram
    • Work Backward • Solve a Simpler Problem

Choose a strategy and solve.

5. A circular area in a park has a radius of 40 feet. The area is to be covered with sod that costs $0.25 per square foot. How much will the sod cost?

6. The edge of a flower bed is 16 feet long. It is lined with 8-inch bricks laid end to end. How many bricks are needed?

WRITER'S CORNER

7. Write your own problem using the formula $R = \frac{Ph}{3} - w$. Solve.

Solid Figures (Polyhedra)

Write *pyramid* or *prism* to describe each polyhedron. Then write
the specific name for each.

1. one rectangular base; other faces, triangles

_____ ; _____

2. four congruent triangles

_____ ; _____

3. one pentagonal base; other faces, triangles

_____ ; _____

4. two congruent parallel hexagonal bases; other faces, parallelograms

_____ ; _____

Describe each polyhedron. Include the shape of the base, or
bases, and the shape of the other faces.

5. square prism

_____

_____

6. triangular prism

_____

_____

7. rectangular prism

_____

_____

Mixed Applications

8. Mike's fish tank is a prism with a pentagonal base, each side measuring 8 inches. What is the base perimeter of his fish tank?

_____

9. Alice wants to build a box for her TV. Which design is better: a rectangular prism or a rectangular pyramid? Explain.

_____

_____

VISUAL THINKING

10. Write the letter of the polyhedron that can be made from this pattern.

_____

a. pentagonal prism

b. square prism

c. octagonal pyramid

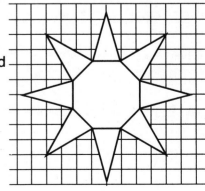

Cylinders, Cones, and Spheres

Write *cylinder, cone,* or *sphere* to identify the geometric figure.
Two views are shown for each figure.

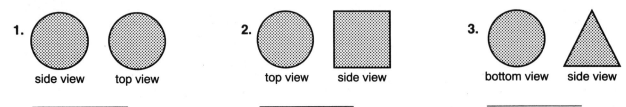

1. side view   top view

_____

2. top view   side view

_____

3. bottom view   side view

_____

Write *cylinder, cone,* or *sphere* for each description.

4. one curved surface, no flat surfaces

_____

5. one curved surface, one flat surface

_____

Write *cylinder, cone,* or *sphere* to identify the described
geometric figure or figures. Explain.

6. ideal shape for a pencil

_____

7. ideal shape for a tennis ball

_____

Mixed Applications

8. Tammy wants to make a cylindrical
container for tennis balls with a
diameter equal to 2.5 inches. What is
the minimum circumference of a can in
which the balls could be stacked on top
of each other?

_____

9. A rocket consists of a cylindrical body
and a conical top. If the circumference
of the base of the cone is 2 inches
greater than the 19-inch circumference
of the body, what is the radius of the
base of the cone?

_____

SCIENCE CONNECTION

Give the circumference of the following. Round your answers to
the nearest hundredth.

10. Earth has a radius of 6.36×10^6 m.

_____

11. The radius of the moon's orbit around the sun is 3.82×10^8 m.

_____

12. The earth's radius of orbit around the sun is 1.50×10^{11} m.

_____

Exploring Three-Dimensional Drawings

Use one-point perspective to draw each view. Do not show hidden lines.

1. Draw a right view.

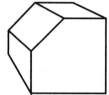

2. Draw a left view.

Use one-point perspective to draw each view.

3. Draw a left view.

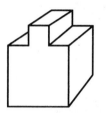

4. Draw a right view.

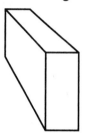

Mixed Applications

5. How many cubes with a 1-inch edge are needed to make a rectangular prism with dimensions 4 inches by 5 inches by 2 inches? to make a cube with a 3-inch edge?

6. After her vacation, Judy wanted to show her teacher a right view of the two L's in the HOLLYWOOD sign in California. Draw the picture for her. (Omit hidden lines.)

VISUAL THINKING

7. Draw any three-dimensional object from either a left or right perspective. Then try to draw the opposite perspective of your drawing.

Surface Area of Prisms and Pyramids

Find the surface area of each prism or pyramid.

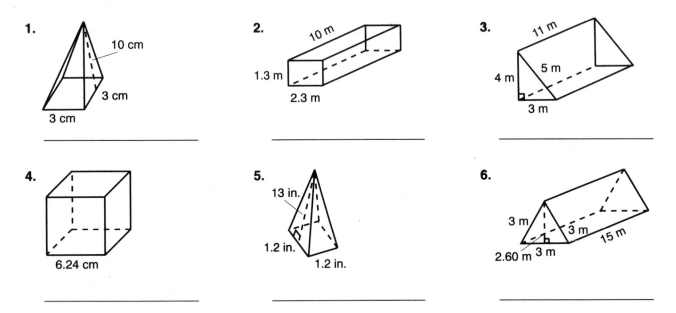

1. 10 cm   3 cm   3 cm

2. 10 m   1.3 m   2.3 m

3. 11 m   5 m   4 m   3 m

4. 6.24 cm

5. 13 in.   1.2 in.   1.2 in.

6. 3 m   3 m   15 m   2.60 m   3 m

Find the surface area. Round to the nearest tenth.

Mixed Applications

7. Suzanne and Corey have plans to build a tent. The tent is to be a pyramid with a hexagonal base 3 m on a side, and with a slant height of 7.5 m. How much material do they need to buy if all sides (not including the base) are to be covered?

8. Jackie wants to paint the walls of her living room. The room is 30 ft long by 15 ft wide by 12 ft high. If 1 gallon of paint is enough to paint 280 square ft, how many gallons will she need?

SOCIAL STUDIES CONNECTION

9. The Great Pyramid, built for King Khufu, measures 755 feet on a side. It was so perfectly arranged that each of its corners was exactly aligned with one of the four cardinal points (north, south, east, and west). This towering mass soared almost 500 ft into the sky. About how much exposed surface area is there, assuming the surfaces were flat? (HINT: slant height = 626.5 feet.)

Exploring Surface Area of Cylinders and Cones

Complete these formulas for surface area.

1. $S_{cone} = \pi r^2 +$ _____

2. $S_{cylinder} =$ _____ $\pi r^2 +$ _____ πr _____

3. Find the surface area of a cone with 5 cm slant height and a 3 cm radius. _____

Find the surface area. Use $\pi = 3.14$. Round to the nearest tenth.

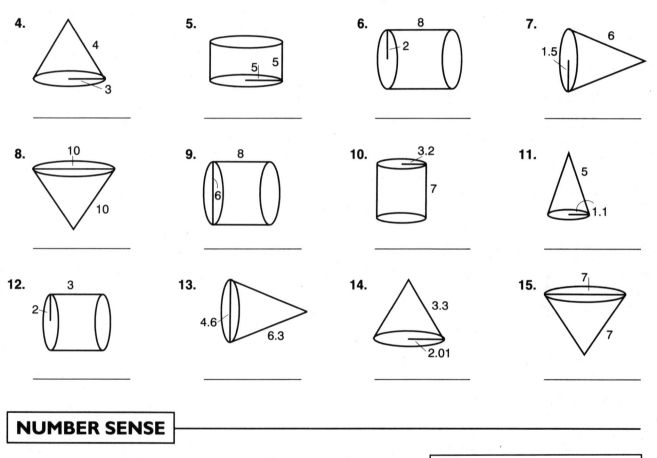

4. 4 3

_____

5. 5 5

_____

6. 8 2

_____

7. 6 1.5

_____

8. 10 10

_____

9. 8 6

_____

10. 3.2 7

_____

11. 5 1.1

_____

12. 3 2

_____

13. 4.6 6.3

_____

14. 3.3 2.01

_____

15. 7 7

_____

NUMBER SENSE

These two sentences will help you find the numerical value of π to six decimal places.

> Pie.
> I wish I could calculate Pie.

16. What is the value of π to 6 decimal places? (HINT: Count the number of letters in each word, in sequence.)

_____

Volume of Prisms and Pyramids

Find each volume.

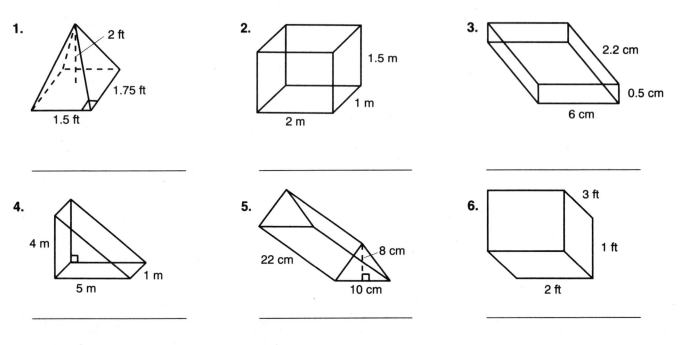

1. 2 ft / 1.75 ft / 1.5 ft

_____

2. 1.5 m / 1 m / 2 m

_____

3. 2.2 cm / 0.5 cm / 6 cm

_____

4. 4 m / 5 m / 1 m

_____

5. 22 cm / 8 cm / 10 cm

_____

6. 3 ft / 1 ft / 2 ft

_____

Find the volume of the shaded portion.

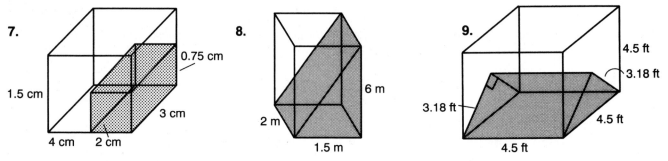

7. 0.75 cm / 1.5 cm / 3 cm / 4 cm / 2 cm

_____

8. 6 m / 2 m / 1.5 m

_____

9. 4.5 ft / 3.18 ft / 3.18 ft / 4.5 ft / 4.5 ft

_____

Mixed Applications

10. A box has a volume of 1,000 cm³. If the box is a cube, what are its dimensions?

_____

11. If a square pyramid has a volume of 91.1 ft³ and a height of 7 ft, what is the length of a side of the base?

_____

LOGICAL REASONING

12. How could you quickly determine the volume of a square pyramid with height equal to twice the side of its base?

_____

Volume of Cylinders and Cones

Find the volume. Use π = 3.14, and round to the nearest whole number.

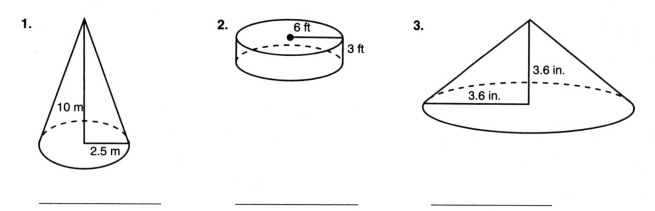

1. 10 m 2.5 m

2. 6 ft 3 ft

3. 3.6 in. 3.6 in.

_____   _____   _____

Find the volume of the shaded portion. Round to the nearest
whole number.

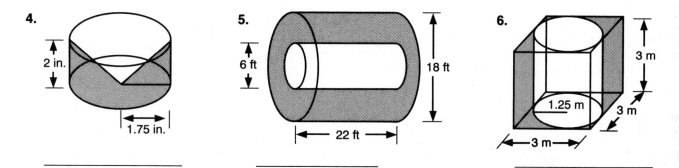

4. 2 in. 1.75 in.

5. 6 ft 18 ft 22 ft

6. 3 m 3 m 3 m 1.25 m

_____   _____   _____

Mixed Applications

7. A cone has a radius of 3 m, a height of
4 m, and a slant height of 5 m. What is
the volume of the cone?

_____

8. A cylindrical gas tank has a volume of
1,808.64 m³. Its height is 9 m. What is
its radius?

_____

MIXED REVIEW

Find the surface area. Round to the nearest tenth.

1. cube of side 3.2 in.

_____

2. square pyramid with side 2.1 cm.; slant
height 4.4 cm.

_____

Capacity

Each statement is about water. Complete.

1. 6.7 cm³ = _____ mL

2. 3.2 kg has a volume of _____ L

Find the capacity of each and the mass of the water it can hold to the nearest tenth.

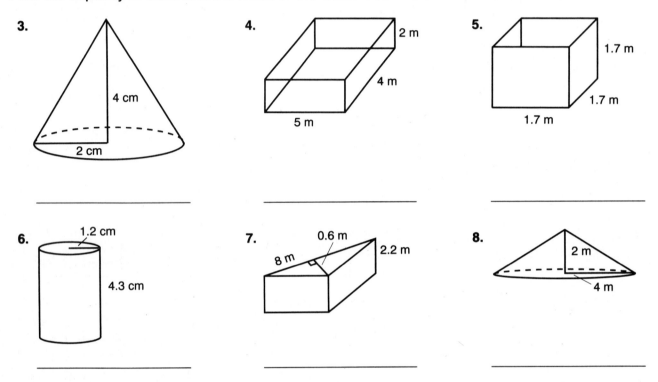

3. 4 cm   2 cm

_____

4. 2 m   4 m   5 m

_____

5. 1.7 m   1.7 m   1.7 m

_____

6. 1.2 cm   4.3 cm

_____

7. 0.6 m   8 m   2.2 m

_____

8. 2 m   4 m

_____

Mixed Applications

9. A cylindrical bucket, with diameter 10 cm and height 15 cm, was left out in a rainstorm. The bucket was $\frac{2}{3}$ full. How much does the water weigh?

_____

10. An ice cube tray can hold 20 ice cubes of dimensions 2.75 cm × 5 cm × 2.25 cm. If the tray weighs 86 grams, how much will the tray full of water weigh?

_____

LOGICAL REASONING

11. A cylindrical container holds 900 L of a liquid. If the diameter of the cylinder were diminished by $\frac{2}{3}$, what volume of liquid will the new container hold?

_____

Problem-Solving Strategy
Use a Formula

Use the formula $V = \frac{4}{3}\pi r^3$ for Exercises 1–4.

1. A tennis ball has a diameter of 6.5 cm. A soccer ball has a 22-cm diameter. How many tennis balls would it take to exceed the volume of a soccer ball?

   _____

2. Darren's inflated balloon can reach a diameter of 9 cm. If Darren fills his balloon with water, how much will it weigh?

   _____

3. A sphere will fit perfectly in a cube 6 in. on a side. What is the volume of the cube less that of the sphere?

   _____

4. How many oranges of radius 4.5 cm will fit in a box 27 cm by 81 cm by 9 cm?

   _____

Mixed Applications	**STRATEGIES**	• Make a Table • Use a Formula • Use an Equation • Draw a Diagram

Choose a strategy and solve.

5. Kelly can shovel snow off a 20 ft by 8 ft driveway in 43 min. How long will it take her to shovel a driveway that is 15 ft by 15 ft?

   _____

6. Juanita is saving 40% of her weekly earnings to buy a bike. If the bike costs $215, how much must she earn to have enough for the bike?

   _____

7. Susan has four times as many pennies as dimes and one third as many quarters as pennies. If she has 38 coins, how much does she have?

   _____

8. If 12.3 L per minute will flow through a water faucet, about how long will it take to fill a cylinder with radius 4 meters, and height 12 meters halfway?

   _____

EVERYDAY MATH CONNECTION

9. Jon can carry 25 pounds in the basket on his bicycle. 23 pages in a newspaper weigh about 1 pound. If today's issue of the newspaper has 76 pages, and Jon has to deliver papers to 33 different houses, how many trips must Jon make to pick up his papers and carry them to his house?

   _____

Exploring Right Triangles

Name the hypotenuse and the legs of each right triangle.

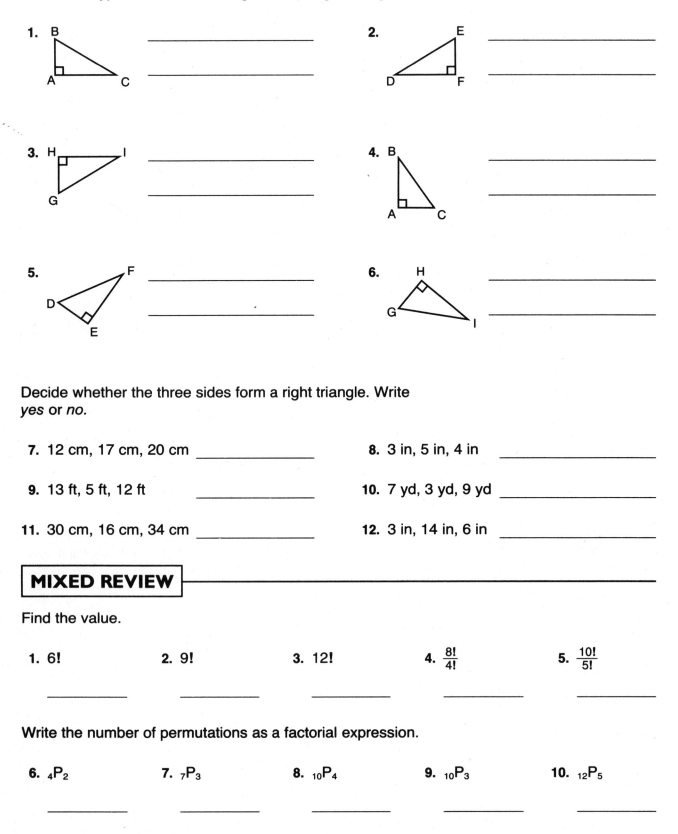

1. B _____

A ⌐ C _____

2. E _____

D F _____

3. H I _____

G _____

4. B _____

A C _____

5. F _____

D E _____

6. H _____

G I _____

Decide whether the three sides form a right triangle. Write
yes or *no.*

7. 12 cm, 17 cm, 20 cm _____

8. 3 in, 5 in, 4 in _____

9. 13 ft, 5 ft, 12 ft _____

10. 7 yd, 3 yd, 9 yd _____

11. 30 cm, 16 cm, 34 cm _____

12. 3 in, 14 in, 6 in _____

MIXED REVIEW

Find the value.

1. 6!

2. 9!

3. 12!

4. $\frac{8!}{4!}$

5. $\frac{10!}{5!}$

_____ _____ _____ _____ _____

Write the number of permutations as a factorial expression.

6. $_4P_2$

7. $_7P_3$

8. $_{10}P_4$

9. $_{10}P_3$

10. $_{12}P_5$

_____ _____ _____ _____ _____

Using the Pythagorean Property

Find the unknown length to the nearest tenth.

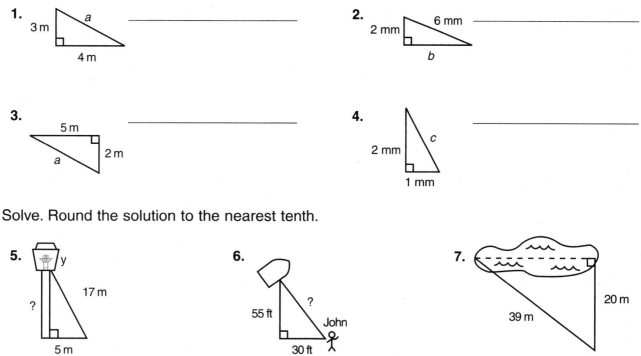

1.   3 m   a   4 m   _____

2.   2 mm   6 mm   b   _____

3.   5 m   2 m   a   _____

4.   2 mm   c   1 mm   _____

Solve. Round the solution to the nearest tenth.

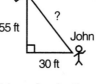

5.   y   17 m   ?   5 m

How high is the
lamppost?

_____

6.   55 ft   ?   John   30 ft

How far is the
boat from John?

_____

7.   20 m   39 m

What is the length
of the pond?

_____

Mixed Applications

8. John's kite is 45 ft above the ground.
A tree is directly under the kite. John is
standing 12 ft away from the tree. How
long is the kite string?

_____

9. Meg is 4 years older than Steve, who is
twice as old as Pat. If Meg is 24, how
old is Pat?

_____

WRITER'S CORNER

10. Use the drawing to write a problem of your own. Solve.

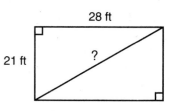

28 ft

21 ft   ?

_____

_____

Exploring Special Right Triangles

Use Figure *A* to find the unknown length.

1. $a = 5$, $c =$ _____

2. $a = 7$, $c =$ _____

3. $c = 3$, $b =$ _____

4. $c = 12$, $a =$ _____

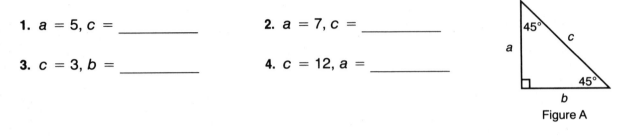

Figure A

Use Figure *B* to find the unknown length.

5. $c = 6$, $a =$ _____

6. $c = 4$, $b =$ _____

7. $c = 10$, $b =$ _____

8. $a = 9$, $c =$ _____

Figure B

Mixed Applications

9. About how high is the kite?

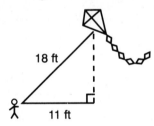

18 ft

11 ft

10. A telephone pole is 45 ft tall. A guy wire is attached to the top of the pole and makes a 45° angle with the ground. What is the length of the guy wire?

_____

_____

MIXED REVIEW

Compute the answers.

1. $4 + {}^-13 =$ _____

2. $^-3 + {}^-11 =$ _____

3. $^-17 + 5 =$ _____

4. $41 + {}^-5 =$ _____

5. $^-30 - 12 =$ _____

6. $^-7 - {}^-12 =$ _____

7. $8 - {}^-8 =$ _____

8. $^-4 - {}^-4 =$ _____

Problem Solving
Making Decisions

Jill's family found three places to stay on their vacation.

Choice 1: The cost is $55 per night.

Choice 2: The cost is $70 per night, breakfast included.

Choice 3: The cost is $50 per night plus $2 per night for parking.

Use the choices listed above for Exercises 1–4.

1. What is the difference in the costs of Choice 1 and Choice 2?

2. Which choice will have the lowest cost for 5 nights?

3. Suppose Jill and her family decide on Choice 3. How much will they pay for parking if they stay 7 nights?

4. Which choice do you think Jill and her family should make? Give reasons.

Mixed Applications ⟩ **STRATEGIES** | • Draw a Diagram • Work Backward • Write an Equation • Use a Formula

Choose a strategy and solve.

5. John leaves to go to town, 14 mi away. At the same time John's brother leaves town to go home. John walks 4 mph, and his brother walks 3 mph. How far from home will they be when they meet?

6. Marta wants to know how many gifts of from $10 to $15 she can buy. She also needs $15 for a train ticket home. She has $95 and wants to keep $10. How many gifts can she get?

SOCIAL STUDIES CONNECTION

7. The Sears Tower in Chicago is 1,454 feet tall. Write a problem using this fact and the Pythagorean Property. Solve.

Similar Figures

Tell whether the figures in each pair are similar. Write *yes* or *no*.

1.

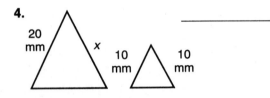

_____

2.

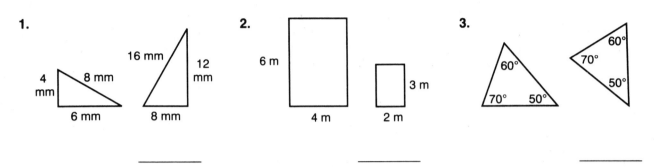

_____

3.

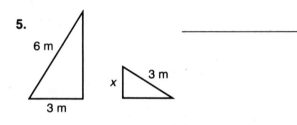

_____

The triangles in each pair are similar. Find *x*.

4.

20 mm /\ *x* 10 mm /\ 10 mm

_____

5.

6 m /| *x* /| 3 m, 3 m

_____

Mixed Applications

6. Joe is making a map of a building. The actual size of the building is 200 m long by 50 m wide. His map is 1 m long by 0.25 m wide. Is Joe's map in proportion?

_____

7. A fruit basket has a combined total of 14 apples, oranges, and pears. If the probability of choosing an apple without looking is $\frac{5}{14}$, how many apples are in the basket?

_____

LOGICAL REASONING

8. Similar triangles are used to find distances in surveying. Describe how you may be able to use a small ruler and similar triangles to calculate the distance from a flag pole. The following diagram may help.

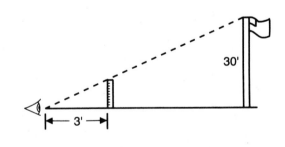

_____

_____

Core Skills: Math, Grade 8, Answer Key

Page 1

1. twenty thousand, one hundred seven
2. fifty-two thousand, thirty-seven and two tenths
3. hundreds
4. ten-thousandths
5. 2,010
6. 8,700,000
7. 35.842 million
8. 60 million
9. >
10. >
11. =
12. 14,300,000
13. Answers will vary.
14. 45,123

Page 2

1. tens
2. tenths
3. thousands
4. hundredths
5. hundreds
6. millions
7. tenths
8. hundreds
9. thousandths
10. 234; 225
11. 4,249; 4,150
12. 56,499; 55,500
13. 8,499; 7,500
14. 654; 645
15. 7,454,999; 7,445,000
16. 3,849,999; 3,750,000
17. 2,374,999; 2,365,000
18. 124,999,999; 115,000,000
19. 3,100,000; 3.1 million
20. 24,400,000; 24.4 million
21. 185,800,000; 185.8 million
22. 607,600,000; 607.6 million
23. 2,365,200,000; 2,365.2 million
24. 5,000,700,000; 5,000.7 million
25. 4,500,000
26. 15.5

Page 3

1. a
2. a
3. b
4. b
5. a
6. b
7–10. Estimates will vary. Exact answers are given for comparison.
7. 106
8. 1,872
9. 7,027
10. 11.5
11. underestimate
12. underestimate
13. Check problems.

Page 4

1. Commutative Property of Addition
2. Distributive Property
3. Associative Property of Multiplication
4. Identity Property (Property of 0)
5. Commutative Property of Multiplication
6. Identity Property (Property of 1)
7. Distributive Property
8. 0
9. 1
10. 25, 60, 77
11. $(4 \times 0.90) + (4 \times 0.15) = 4 \times (0.90 + 0.15) = 4 \times 1.05 = 4.20$; $4.20
12. $(21 + 9) + 47 = 30 + 47 = 77$

Mixed Review

1. <
2. >
3. 15.0
4. 134.7

Page 5

1. about $130; $131.39
2. about $4; $4.28
3. about 4 min; 4.26 min
4. about 200 km; 177 km
5. about $1,050; $1,037.25
6. about 5,500 miles; 5,479 miles
7. $3.98
8. $399.45
9. $498.97
10. $1,130.10

Page 6

1. Find amount remaining; divide by $3. 56 subscriptions
2. Subtract the readings; divide by 2. 113.65 mi
3. Multiply $5 by 4; add $12. $32
4. Add $100 to previous balance; subtract checks. $274.58
5. $21.89
6. $511.15
7. Check problem.

Page 7

1. 728 passengers
2. $32.75
3. $32.45 each
4. $10,299.82
5. $96.25 in all
6. 29 bags
7. $380 for 5 nights
8. 5 cans
9. 3, 7, 5
10. 1, 2, 5, 8, 9

Page 8

1. 19
2. 15
3. 0.36
4. 59
5. 21
6. 2.2
7. 79
8. 6.1
9. 6.4
10. 24.5
11. 18.9
12. 9.1
13. 2.4
14. 20.4
15. 3.8
16. 160.9
17. 5.49
18. 6.85
19. 0.06
20. 2.29
21. 0.54
22. 11.67
23. 25.63
24. 21.72
25. $68.41
26. 5 times greater
27. Possible answer: 1 half dollar, 1 quarter, 4 dimes, 4 pennies

Page 9

1. $13 \frac{1}{3}$ mi apart
2. 6 boats
3. 5 tickets
4. 6 tokens
5. 4 packs
6. $3 \frac{1}{8}$ gal
7. 11.8 gal
8. Write remainder as a whole number.
9. He multiplied both the divisor and dividend by 100, so the remainder was also multiplied by 100. He had $7 left.

Page 10

1. 2^3
2. 5^4
3. 6^2
4. 4^4
5. 7^3
6. 14^2
7. 1^5
8. 10^3
9. 1.8^4
10. 128
11. 729
12. 49
13. 1
14. 4
15. 16
16. 2,401

Page 10 (cont.)
17. 13
18. 25
19. 1
20. 1,296
21. 625
22. 9
23. 7
24. 16
25. 8
26. 4
27. 0
28. 1
29. 0
30. 3
31. 2
32. 9
33. 10
34. 5
35. 3
36. 1
37. 13
38. 32.768 cm³
39. 9 days
Mixed Review
1. 8.8
2. 1,200,000

Page 11
1. 45
2. 6
3. 42
4. 5
5. 8
6. 34
7. 3
8. 27
9. 12
10. 15
11. 6
12. 32
13. 6
14. 6
15. 16
16. 53
17. 5
18. 39
19. 216
20. 567
21. 1
22. $4 \times 3.2 = +12 = 24.8$
23. $20 - 5.5 = x\,2.5 = 36.25$
24. $4 \times 2 + 3^2 - 1 = 16$
25. $6 \times 3 - 3^2 = 9$
26.

Page 12
1. expression
2. equation
3. inequality
4. equation
5–7. Examples will vary.
8. >
9. =

Page 12 (cont.)
10. >
11. <
12–19. Answers will vary.
12. $513 + 23 = 536$
13. $15 \times 4 - 20 = 40$
14. $d + 18 = 30$
15. $\frac{a}{6} - 7 = 9$
16. $33 - 7 > 16$
17. $16.5 + 8.5 < 50$
18. $2x + 3 \le 13$
19. $c - 10 \ge 5$
20. 12×3
21. $12 \div 4 = 3$
22. $12 - 9$

Page 13
1. $c + 12$
2. $m + 5$
3. $s - 16$
4. $a - 33$
5–6. Expressions will vary.
7. 14.5
8. 2
9. 15
10. 7
11. 25
12. 34.5
13. 5.5
14. 6
15. $p + 20$
16. $r - 3.25$
17. 40

Page 14
1. yes
2. no
3. yes
4. $s = 53$
5. $q = 26$
6. $n = 26$
7. $y = 52$
8–9. Possible variable is given.
8. $d =$ number of days worked;
   $d + 8 = 32$
9. $b =$ cost of a backpack;
   $b + \$38.55 = \$198.17$
10. $x + 95 = 220$; $x = 125$; $125
11. $x + 3.39 = 48.87$, $x = 45.48$;
    $45.48
12. Check problem.

Page 15
1. 12 dimes
2. 16 postcards
3. 20 packages
4. 4 dimes
5. 22 letters
6. 7 quarters
7. 8 girls
8. $0.89
9. 62 Perseids

Page 16
1. $m = 38$
2. $k = 77$
3. $z = 75$

Page 16 (cont.)
4. $w = 84$
5. $g = 68$
6. $t = 11.4$
7. $s = 6.1$
8. $r = 29$
9–10. Variables will vary.
9. $b =$ number of band
   instruments; $b - 10 = 47$
10. $m =$ number of meters;
    $m - 25.6 = 84.3$
11. $r - 55 = 248$; $r = 303$; $303
12. $m - 4 = 11$; $m = 15$; $15 + x =$
    53; $x = 38$; 38 years old
Mixed Review
1. 58
2. 22
3. 4
4. 1
5. $x = 21$
6. $c = 47$
7. $y = 1.7$
8. $z = 0$

Page 17
1. $3a$
2. $2l$
3. $\frac{p}{8}$
4. $\frac{d}{7}$
5. $15m$
6. $\frac{h}{24}$
7. Word expressions will vary.
8. 30
9. 9
10. 19.2
11. 0.2
12. 0.5
13. 12
14. 0.4
15. 10
16. $0.99b$
17. $\frac{4n}{6}$ or $4\left(\frac{n}{6}\right)$
18. 1

Page 18
1. $n = 8$
2. $x = 47$
3. $q = 52$
4. $r = 3$
5. $t = 15$
6. $s = 125$
7. $p = 10.4$
8. $b = 20$
9. $k = 4$
10. $m = 50$
11. $j = 0.6$
12. $y = 4$
13. $s = 123$
14. $a = 23.6$
15. $c = 25.8$
16. $k = 86$
17. $e = 32$
18. $h = 0.4$
19. $n = 8$
20. $t = 3$

Page 18 (cont.)

21. $9x = 1{,}308.24$; $x = 145.36$; $145.36
22. $3 per hour
23. 0.125 cm^3

Page 19

1. multiplication
2. division
3. subtraction
4. addition
5. $w = 24$
6. $n = 63$
7. $x = 170$
8. $b = 216$
9. $y = 2.32$
10. $k = 25.2$
11. $d = 148$
12. $c = 68$
13. $n = 10.34$
14. $a = 256$
15. $y = 49$
16. $h = 744$
17. $\frac{n}{5} = 15.5$; $n = 77.5$; $77.50
18. $30n = 120$; $n = 4$; 4 persons

Mixed Review

1. $x = 13$
2. $y = 72$
3. $b = 4.7$
4. $x = 8$
5. $k = 7.2$
6. $p = 55$
7. $l = 44$
8. $m = 95$

Page 20

1. subtraction; multiplication
2. addition; division
3. addition; multiplication
4. subtraction; division
5. $x = 25$
6. $d = 162$
7. $w = 4$
8. $c = 3$
9. $b = 4$
10. $a = 3$
11. $t = 24$
12. $k = 3$
13. $11c - 7 = 70$
14. $\frac{n}{8} + 4 = 28$
15. $2w - 10 = 35$; $w = 22.5$; 22.5 ft
16. $0.0625 + 0.625 \times 2.4$
17. $t + 3t + 8t = 180$; 15°, 45°, 120°

Page 21

1. $a < 5$; 0, 1, 2, 3, 4
2. $b \le 7$; 0, 1, 2, 3, 4, 5, 6, 7
3. $c \ge 7$; 7, 8, 9, . . .
4. $d > 4$; 5, 6, 7, . . .
5. $k \ge 9$; 9, 10, 11, . . .
6. $x < 3$; 0, 1, 2
7. $n \ne 3$; all whole numbers except 3
8. $5 > y$; 0, 1, 2, 3, 4
9. $p \ge 13$; 13, 14, 15, . . .
10. $a - 30 < 450$; $a < 480$; less than $480

Page 21 (cont.)

11. $6w < 828$; $w < 138$; no, each was paid less than $138.
12. False; "more than 12" means 13, 14, 15, . . .
13. Cannot tell; the total number of games played is not given.

Page 22

1–6. Variables will vary.

1. $x + 587.46 = 675$; $x = 87.54$; $87.54
2. $3s = 225$; $s = 75$; $75
3. $l + 4.7 = 7$; $l = 2.3$; 2.3 T more
4. $p - 76 = 1897$; $p = 1973$; 1973
5. $4k = 2.4$; $k = 0.6$; 0.6 gal
6. $\frac{d}{12} = 12.50$; $d = 150$; $150
7. 7 quarters and 3 dimes
8. no
9. $1,245
10. 79 cameras

Page 23

1. prime
2. prime
3. composite
4. prime
5. composite
6. composite
7. 2×3^2
8. 2×17
9. $2^4 \times 3$
10. $2^3 \times 7$
11. 2^4
12. $2^3 \times 3^2$
13. 2×3^3
14. 2×29
15. $2^2 \times 3 \times 5$
16. $2^2 \times 5^2$
17. $2^2 \times 5 \times 7$
18. $2^3 \times 5^2$
19. 18
20. 315
21. 2,200
22. 735
23. 1,925
24. 76
25. 72
26. 2,079
27. 1,040
28. 9 choices
29. 23 and 29
30. 4, 9, 25, 49

Page 24

1. 42 days
2. 3 in.
3. 12 vases
4. 40 min
5. 36 Venus's-flytraps
6. 42 in.

Mixed Review

1. $u = 47$
2. $a = 362$
3. $n = 26$
4. $x = 448$
5. $2^3 \times 3$

Page 24 (cont.)

6. 2^5
7. 2×29

Page 25

1. $80
2. $154.40
3. $95.60; $79.40
4. Answers and reasons will vary.
5. about $800
6. $49

Page 26

1–4. Fractions may vary.

1. $\frac{6}{16}, \frac{9}{24}, \frac{12}{32}$
2. $\frac{4}{10}, \frac{6}{15}, \frac{8}{20}$
3. $\frac{10}{24}, \frac{15}{36}, \frac{20}{48}$
4. $\frac{22}{42}, \frac{33}{63}, \frac{44}{84}$
5. $\frac{1}{8}$
6. $\frac{1}{2}$
7. $\frac{1}{3}$
8. $\frac{1}{2}$
9. $\frac{1}{4}$
10. $6\frac{3}{7}$
11. $8\frac{1}{3}$
12. $4\frac{3}{4}$
13. $4\frac{1}{5}$
14. 3
15. $\frac{8}{3}$
16. $\frac{24}{7}$
17. $\frac{41}{6}$
18. $\frac{29}{8}$
19. $\frac{32}{5}$
20. rock: $\frac{8}{16}$ or $\frac{1}{2}$; country: $\frac{2}{16}$ or $\frac{1}{8}$; jazz: $\frac{6}{16}$ or $\frac{3}{8}$
21. $20\frac{1}{4}$
22. Top: $\frac{13}{5}, \frac{18}{5}, \frac{23}{5}$; Bottom: $2\frac{1}{5}$, $2\frac{4}{5}$, 3, 4, $4\frac{4}{5}$

Page 27

1. 12
2. 14
3. 60
4. 30
5. $<$
6. $>$
7. $>$
8. $<$
9. $>$
10. $>$
11. $=$
12. $<$
13. $\frac{3}{8}, \frac{1}{2}, \frac{2}{3}$
14. $\frac{11}{25}, \frac{7}{10}, \frac{7}{9}$
15. $2\frac{1}{3}; 2\frac{5}{12}; 2\frac{1}{2}$
16. $\frac{4}{5}, \frac{7}{4}, 1\frac{9}{10}$

Page 27 (cont.)
17. the group that spent 20 min per day
18. 2.2, $\frac{7}{3}$, 2.4, $2\frac{3}{4}$, $2\frac{7}{9}$

Mixed Review
1. 2^4
2. $2^3 \times 3$
3. $2^3 \times 7$
4. $\frac{2}{3}$
5. $\frac{3}{5}$
6. $\frac{1}{3}$
7. $\frac{7}{20}$
8. $\frac{4}{3}$
9. $\frac{2}{7}$
10. $\frac{8}{11}$
11. $\frac{7}{3}$

Page 28
1. a
2. c
3. b
4–7. Estimates may vary.
4. 1
5. $\frac{1}{2}$
6. 20
7. 8
8. about 5 oz
9. No; an estimate of the difference is 1, and $\frac{13}{5}$ is more than 2.
10. about $2\frac{1}{2}$; about $2.50 higher

Page 29
1. $\frac{3}{5}$
2. $\frac{10}{15} = \frac{2}{3}$
3. $\frac{7}{8}$
4. $\frac{5}{6}$
5. $\frac{25}{36}$
6. $19\frac{5}{9}$
7. $7\frac{19}{20}$
8. $5\frac{10}{9} = 6\frac{1}{9}$
9. $11\frac{13}{20}$
10. $10\frac{13}{15}$
11. $3\frac{19}{20}$
12. $17\frac{5}{8}$
13. $\frac{17}{15} = 1\frac{2}{15}$
14. $\frac{7}{18}$
15. $13\frac{13}{14}$
16. $15\frac{5}{6}$ hr
17. $763\frac{7}{20}$ gal
18. Possible answers: $\frac{3}{4} = \frac{1}{2} + \frac{1}{4}$; $\frac{8}{15} = \frac{1}{3} + \frac{1}{5}$; $\frac{7}{12} = \frac{1}{4} + \frac{1}{3}$; $\frac{2}{3} = \frac{1}{2} + \frac{1}{6}$; $\frac{1}{2} = \frac{1}{3} + \frac{1}{6}$

Page 30
1. $\frac{2}{7}$
2. $\frac{5}{36}$
3. $\frac{31}{60}$
4. $6\frac{7}{18}$
5. $4\frac{5}{8}$
6. 3
7. 3
8. $\frac{7}{10}$
9. $\frac{3}{8}$
10. $8\frac{1}{24}$
11. $\frac{5}{12}$
12. 1
13. $69\frac{1}{30}$ hr
14. $\frac{1}{4}$

Mixed Review
1. <
2. >
3. >
4. =
5–8. Estimates will vary.
5. 11,000
6. 6
7. 12
8. $\frac{1}{2}$

Page 31
1. $9\frac{7}{8}$ ft away from each width; $17\frac{5}{8}$ ft from each length
2. 4 sections
3. 2 blocks
4. 44 cows
5. about 11 hr
6. 8 dimes and 3 nickels
7. $5\frac{1}{4}$ ft
8. $93

Page 32
1–17. Estimates may vary. Possible estimates are given.
1. $\frac{1}{2}$
2. 1
3. 6
4. 12
5. 36
6. 20
7. 32
8. 10
9. 72
10. 4
11. 6
12. [64]; close estimate
13. [30]; underestimate
14. [1]; overestimate
15. [10]; close estimate
16. [50]; overestimate
17. [64]; close estimate
18. about 45 acres
19. about $50

Page 32 (cont.)
20. Possible estimates are: 1 c; 1 tsp; $\frac{1}{4}$ c; $\frac{1}{2}$ tbsp

Page 33
1. $\frac{1}{4}$ and $\frac{4}{1}$; $\frac{2}{5}$ and $\frac{5}{2}$
2. $\frac{2}{3}$ and $\frac{3}{2}$; $\frac{1}{9}$ and $\frac{9}{1}$
3. 1
4. $\frac{7}{9}$
5. $\frac{7}{48}$
6. 1
7. 9
8. $\frac{25}{16}$, or $1\frac{9}{16}$
9. $\frac{3}{4}$
10. $\frac{7}{10}$
11. $\frac{4}{21}$
12. 1
13. $\frac{11}{90}$
14. $\frac{3}{8}$
15. $\frac{5}{24}$
16. $\frac{4}{5}$
17. 8 palm trees
18. $\frac{11}{12}$ of the garden
19. $\frac{1}{25}$
20. $\frac{4}{9}$
21. $\frac{8}{125}$
22. $\frac{1}{81}$

Page 34
1. 45
2. $\frac{44}{45}$
3. $\frac{36}{11}$, or $3\frac{3}{11}$
4. $18\frac{2}{3}$
5. 26
6. $6\frac{1}{3}$
7. $34\frac{2}{3}$
8. $35\frac{13}{20}$
9. $34\frac{3}{8}$
10. $1\frac{5}{16}$
11. $1\frac{83}{160}$
12. 0.25, or $\frac{1}{4}$
13. 0.375, or $\frac{3}{8}$
14. 4.275, or $4\frac{11}{40}$
15. Possible answers: $2\frac{1}{2} \times 3\frac{3}{20}$, $1\frac{1}{2} \times 5\frac{1}{4}$
16. $27\frac{1}{2}$ lb
17. $9\frac{27}{32}$ hr

Mixed Review
1–8. Estimates may vary.
1. 1,800
2. 104

Page 34 (cont.)
3. 1
4. 40
5. 1.5
6. 32
7. 2
8. 77

Page 35
1. greater than 1
2. less than 1
3. less than 1
4. greater than 1
5. less than 1
6. greater than 1
7. greater than 1
8. less than 1
9. less than 1
10. greater than 1
11. greater than 1
12. less than 1
13–21. Estimates may vary.
13. 3
14. 2
15. $\frac{1}{2}$
16. 1
17. 8
18. $\frac{2}{3}$
19. 4
20. $\frac{1}{3}$
21. $\frac{1}{5}$
22. about 20 plants
23. about 8 lb
24. $\frac{1}{8}$

Page 36
1. $\frac{5}{4}$, or $1\frac{1}{4}$
2. 10
3. $\frac{119}{108}$, or $1\frac{11}{108}$
4. $\frac{1}{10}$
5. $\frac{115}{72}$, or $1\frac{43}{72}$
6. $1\frac{7}{8}$
7. $\frac{10}{81}$
8. $\frac{1}{45}$
9. 16
10. $\frac{1}{48}$
11. $\frac{10}{13}$
12. $\frac{27}{50}$
13. $\frac{1}{6}$
14. $\frac{22}{15}$, or $1\frac{7}{15}$
15. 8 boards; no
16. $4\frac{3}{4}$ cars
17. $\frac{3}{8} \div \frac{1}{4} = 1\frac{1}{2}$
18. $24 \div \frac{4}{9} = 54$
19. $\frac{4}{9} \div \frac{5}{7} = 1\frac{5}{9}$
20. $\frac{2}{3} \div \frac{6}{7} = \frac{7}{9}$
21. $10 \div \frac{5}{12} = 24$

Page 36 (cont.)
22. $\frac{8}{13} \div \frac{2}{7} = 2\frac{2}{13}$

Page 37
1. 15
2. 49
3. 8 people
4. Possible answer: about $290.00
5. $6
6. 27.8 m²
7. Check problem.

Page 38
1. $2\frac{7}{10}$
2. $\frac{23}{24}$
3. $\frac{1}{15}$
4. $2\frac{1}{4}$
5. $4\frac{1}{8}$
6. $4\frac{1}{2}$
7. $\frac{2}{9}$
8. $\frac{25}{184}$
9. $\frac{2}{11}$
10. $1\frac{71}{82}$
11. $\frac{1}{2}$
12. $1\frac{1}{5}$
13. $\frac{3}{5}$
14. $4\frac{14}{15}$
15. $2\frac{11}{32}$
16. 6 servings
17. $1\frac{2}{3}$ ft
18. =
19. ≠
20. =
21. ≠
22. Multiplication is associative; division is not.

Page 39
1. $n = 5$
2. $q = 5\frac{1}{2}$
3. $a = 3\frac{2}{3}$
4. $w = 15\frac{1}{10}$
5. $x = 8$
6. $b = \frac{5}{9}$
7. $t = 4\frac{4}{9}$
8. $t = 2\frac{5}{6}$
9. $z = 41\frac{1}{2}$
10. $r = 1\frac{13}{18}$
11. $h = 3\frac{1}{8}$
12. $k = 37\frac{1}{2}$
13. $12\frac{1}{2}c = 60$; $c = 4.8$; $4.80
14. Divide by 2 or multiply by $\frac{1}{2}$; $\frac{5}{8}, \frac{5}{16}, \frac{5}{32}$

Page 39 (cont.)
Mixed Review
1. <
2. =
3. >
4. =
5. $1\frac{7}{12}$
6. $\frac{7}{30}$
7. $3\frac{2}{15}$
8. $2\frac{2}{5}$

Page 40
1. 0.75
2. 0.7
3. 0.35
4. 0.28125
5. 0.14
6. 0.4
7. 0.3125
8. 0.26
9. 0.625
10. 1.75
11. 0.12
12. 0.85
13. 0.4375
14. $0.\overline{27}$
15. $0.3\overline{8}$
16. $2.\overline{5}$
17. 0.075
18. 3.125
19. $0.3\overline{6}$
20. $0.1\overline{3}$
21. <
22. >
23. =
24. >
25. >
26. =
27. >
28. <
29. 4.875 pages
30. 2.6, $2.\overline{6}$; freestyle event
31. If the prime factors of the denominator of the fraction include only 2s and 5s, the fraction will terminate.

Page 41
1. $\frac{4}{5}$
2. $\frac{3}{25}$
3. $\frac{7}{10}$
4. $\frac{1}{20}$
5. $\frac{3}{40}$
6. $\frac{9}{20}$
7. $\frac{1}{4}$
8. $\frac{1}{50}$
9. $4\frac{1}{2}$
10. $3\frac{47}{50}$
11. $5\frac{6}{25}$
12. $8\frac{9}{25}$
13. $\frac{1}{9}$

145

Page 41 (cont.)
14. $\frac{5}{11}$
15. $\frac{2}{15}$
16. $1\frac{10}{99}$
17. $3\frac{2}{5}$
18. $\frac{41}{50}$
19. $\frac{3}{11}$
20. $1\frac{8}{9}$
21. $0.3, \frac{1}{3}, \frac{2}{5}$
22. $\frac{3}{4}, \frac{5}{6}, \frac{7}{8}, 0.\overline{8}$
23. $0.4, \frac{1}{2}, \frac{6}{11}, 0.\overline{5}$
24. $\frac{1}{4}, \frac{1}{3}, 0.38, 0.45$
25. $1.2, 1.\overline{2}, 1\frac{1}{4}, 1\frac{2}{7}$
26. $0.\overline{1}, \frac{3}{25}, 0.125, \frac{2}{9}$
27. $\frac{7}{20}$ lb
28. Bertha
29. Answers will vary. Possible answer: 0.202002000. . .

Page 42
1. 59 comic books
2. Showanda
3. 9 problems, 4 points; 3 problems, 10 points
4. 100 fish
5. 16 seedlings
6. 3 socks
7. Check problem.

Page 43
1. c
2. a, d
3. e, h
4. b, f, g
5. $\overleftrightarrow{YX}, \overleftrightarrow{YW}, \overleftrightarrow{XW}$
6. $\overline{WX}, \overline{WY}, \overline{XY}$
7. true
8. true
9. true
10. false
11–12. Check drawings.
11. No; a segment is named by its endpoints.
12. $\angle$JKL, $\angle$LKJ, $\angle$K
13. line: 2 points; plane: 3 points

Page 44
1. 15°
2. 123°
3. $m\angle 2 = 54°$, $m\angle 3 = 126°$, $m\angle 4 = 54°$
4–7. Check drawings.
4. 60°, 150°
5. 5°, 95°
6. 65°, 155°
7. 12°, 102°
8. $m\angle 4 = 108°$, $m\angle 6 = 72°$, $m\angle 5 = 108°$

Page 44 (cont.)
9. Possible answers are: $\angle 7$, $\angle 1$; $\angle 2$, $\angle 8$; $\angle 3$, $\angle 5$; $\angle 4$, $\angle 6$; $\angle 3$, $\angle 4$; $\angle 5$, $\angle 6$
10. true

Page 45
1–7. Check constructions.
8. 110°, 70°
9. 5

Page 46
1. 70°
2. 110°
3. 70°
4. 110°
5. 70°
6. 70°
7. parallel
8. perpendicular
9. parallel
10. perpendicular
11. $\angle 5$
12. $\angle 6$
13. $\angle 7$
14. $\angle 8$
15. $\angle 1$ and $\angle 3$, $\angle 2$ and $\angle 4$, $\angle 5$ and $\angle 7$, $\angle 6$ and $\angle 8$
16. $\angle 6$
17. $\angle 5$
18. $\angle 7$
19. $\angle 8$
20. no
21. yes

Page 47
1–4. Check constructions.
3. The lines are parallel.
4. The lines are parallel.
Mixed Review
1. $\frac{1}{5}$
2. $\frac{1}{3}$
3. $\frac{1}{4}$
4. $\frac{1}{8}$
5. $n = 10$
6. $n = 64$
7. $n = 49$
8. $n = 40$

Page 48
1–5. Check constructions.
6. 54 in.
7. $m\angle DEG = 86°$
8. Stu did not open the compass more than $\frac{1}{2}$ the length of the segment.

Page 49
1. b
2. c
3. c
4. [image]
5. 363 and 462
6. Check the problem.

Page 50
1. 180°
2. 1,260°
3. 2,160°
4. 2,520°
5. 3,600°
6. 6,840°
7. 27
8. 54
9. 135
10. [image]
11. [image]
12. [image]
13. [image]
14. 90°: square; 180°: rhombus, square, rectangle
15. 12 cm
16. 135°, 45°, 45°
17. true
18. true
19. false
20. true

Page 51
1. $\angle 2 + \angle 3$
2. $\angle 1 + \angle 3$
3. $\angle 1 + \angle 2$
4. 65°
5. 120°
6. 80°
7. 115°
8. 65°
9. 76°
10. 80°
11. 360°
12. The sum of the measures of the exterior angles of a triangle is 360°.

Page 52
1. $\overline{AB} \cong \overline{MN}$, $\overline{BC} \cong \overline{NO}$, $\overline{CD} \cong \overline{OP}$, $\overline{DA} \cong \overline{PM}$; $\angle A \cong \angle M$, $\angle B \cong \angle N$, $\angle C \cong \angle O$, $\angle D \cong \angle P$
2. $a = 90°$, $b = 8$, $c = 10$
3. $a = 60°$, $b = 12$, $c = 120°$
4. $a = 75°$, $b = 9$, $c = 65°$
5. $a = 80°$, $b = 20$, $c = 15$
6. No; Unless they have corresponding congruent sides as well, they are similar but not congruent.
7. $ABCD$ is a parallelogram.
8. 16

Page 53
1–3. Check constructions.
4. $m\angle E = 120°$, $DE = 6$ cm
5. $m\angle C = 70°$, $m\angle B = 80°$
6. $\triangle PAB \cong \triangle PDC$ by SAS. Thus, $AB = CD$. Mika measures the distance CD on land. This distance will be equal to distance AB.

Page 53 (cont.)

7. Yes; since $\overline{SQ}$ bisects $\angle PSR$, $\angle PSQ \cong \angle RSQ$. $\overline{SQ} \cong \overline{SQ}$ and $\overline{PS} \cong \overline{RS}$. Thus, the triangles are congruent by SAS.

Page 54

1. triangle; 120°
2. quadrilateral; 90°
3. pentagon; 72°
4. hexagon; 60°
5. octagon; 45°
6. 12-sided polygon; 30°
7. Any two of $\angle 1$, $\angle 5$; $\angle 2$, $\angle 6$; $\angle 4$, $\angle 8$; $\angle 3$, $\angle 7$
8. 120°; $\angle 5$ and $\angle 6$ are supplementary.
9. They would all have a measure of 90°.

Mixed Review

1. $1\frac{7}{20}$
2. 10
3. $\frac{9}{14}$
4. $\frac{5}{19}$
5. $\frac{11}{16}$
6. $\frac{1}{5}$
7. $\frac{9}{16}$
8. $\frac{7}{15}$

Page 55

1. $4,357.44
2. $23,357.44
3. $6,631.80
4. $24,631.80
5. Choice 1
6. Choice 3
7–8. Answers will vary.

Page 56

1. $\frac{4}{9}$
2. $\frac{12}{17}$
3. $\frac{5}{8}$
4. $\frac{53}{100}$
5. $\frac{3}{7}$
6. $\frac{3}{5}$
7. $\frac{8}{15}$
8. $\frac{1}{4}$
9. yes
10. no
11. yes
12. no
13. =
14. ≠
15. ≠
16. =
17. ≠
18. ≠
19. =
20. =

Page 56 (cont.)

21. $\frac{\$0.10}{1 \text{ apple}}$
22. $\frac{\$0.05}{1 \text{ oz of cereal}}$
23. $\frac{\$13}{1 \text{ dinner}}$
24. 16 oz of water
25. $\frac{11}{34}$
26. $\frac{1}{4}$
27. $\frac{2}{3}$
28. $\frac{1}{2}$

Page 57

1. $\frac{24}{32} = \frac{3}{4}$
2. $\frac{3}{8} = \frac{69}{184}$
3. $\frac{280}{444} = \frac{70}{111}$
4. $n = 210$
5. $13n = 60$
6. $25n = 32$
7. $100n = 200$
8. $n = 15$
9. $n = 17$
10. $n = 18$
11. $n = 16$
12. $n = 28$
13. $n = 56$
14. $n = 72$
15. $n = 252$
16. $n = 200$
17. $n = 105$
18. $n = 70$
19. $n = 25$
20. $n = 0.18$
21. $n = 2.55$
22. $n = 9.8$
23. $n = 1.96$
24. 12 football fans
25. 21 gal
26. 22 teeth

Page 58

1. 60
2. 135
3. 337.5
4. 5
5. 186
6. 2.6
7. drawing: $3\frac{1}{4}$ in. by $1\frac{1}{2}$ in.; actual: 195 ft by 90 ft
8. drawing: $1\frac{3}{4}$ in. by $\frac{1}{2}$ in.; actual: 105 ft by 30 ft
9. 200 ft by 100 ft
10. 724 stone tiles
11. Check drawing. Rectangle should be 6 cm by 14 cm.

Page 59

1. 85%
2. 42%
3. 12%
4. 9%
5. 93%
6. 79%
7. 3%

Page 59 (cont.)

8. 97%
9. 49%
10. 53%
11. 15%
12. 50%
13. 20%
14. 200%
15. 75%
16. 90%
17. 36%
18. 16%
19. 5%
20. 167%
21. 40%
22. 212.5%
23. 75%
24. 60%
25. extra-small
26. 45%
27. 50%; draw perpendicular dotted lines to show that 4 of 8 congruent triangles are shaded.

Page 60

1. 0.36
2. 0.06
3. 1.35
4. 0.69
5. 0.83
6. 0.75
7. 0.2
8. 0.54
9. 85%
10. 30%
11. 174%
12. 14.5%
13. 125%
14. 8%
15. 51%
16. 1.25%
17. $\frac{91}{100}$
18. $\frac{3}{25}$
19. $\frac{3}{50}$
20. $\frac{93}{100}$
21. $\frac{31}{50}$
22. $\frac{7}{50}$
23. $\frac{7}{10}$
24. $\frac{4}{1}$
25. 60%
26. $33\frac{1}{3}\%$
27. 25%
28. 15%
29. $37\frac{1}{2}\%$
30. 45%
31. 16%
32. 700%
33. 0.02
34. 20%
35. 200%; 2 or 2.00

Page 61
1. 30; 75
2. c
3. a
4. b
5. a
6. Check problem.

Page 62
1. 69
2. 112.5
3. 97.5
4. 828
5. 131.49
6. 2.61
7. 0.189
8. 400
9. 18.333
10. $82.40
11. 24
12. 32
13. 561
14. 0.5
15. 0.6
16. =
17. <
18. 12 jetliners
19. $24.96
Mixed Review
1. $\frac{3}{5}$
2. $\frac{6}{25}$
3. $\frac{1}{50}$
4. $\frac{5}{4}$
5. $\frac{3}{50}$
6. $\frac{2}{5}$
7. $\frac{1}{1}$ or 1
8. $\frac{7}{2}$

Page 63
1. $33\frac{1}{3}$%
2. 75%
3. 80%
4. 15%
5. $33\frac{1}{3}$%
6. 75%
7. $66\frac{2}{3}$%
8. 25%
9. 25%
10. 125%
11. $12\frac{1}{2}$%
12. 30%
13. $37\frac{1}{2}$%
14. $46\frac{2}{3}$%
15. 50%
16. 200%
17. 20%
18. 40%
19. 320%
20. 25%

Page 63 (cont.)
21. $66\frac{2}{3}$%
22. $\frac{3}{8}$
23. Check problem.

Page 64
1. 80
2. 160
3. 720
4. 200
5. 190
6. 200
7. 250
8. 500
9. 670
10. 58
11. 102.5
12. 100
13. 250
14. 2.8
15. 2,500
16. 125
17. 70
18. 220
19. 8,500 students
20. 30.25 hr
Mixed Review
1. $n = 120$
2. $n = 6$
3. $n = 50$
4. 22.5
5. 8.72
6. 1.26

Page 65
1. c
2. a
3. b
4–15. Answers may vary.
4. $\frac{1}{3}$
5. $\frac{3}{4}$
6. $\frac{2}{3}$
7. $\frac{9}{10}$ or $\frac{8}{9}$
8. about 25%
9. about 50%
10. about 75%
11. about $66\frac{2}{3}$%
12. about 50%
13. about 280
14. about 1,600
15. about $33\frac{1}{3}$%
16. 112 seeds
17. +, −

Page 66
1. 800 − 600 = 200; 200/800; $\frac{1}{4}$ = 25%
2. 80% increase
3. 90% decrease
4. $83\frac{1}{3}$% increase
5. 0.4% decrease
6. 200% increase
7. 1,500 more students

Page 67
1. $33\frac{1}{3}$% increase
2. 50% increase
3. 40% decrease
4. 100% increase
5. 62.5% decrease
6. 10% decrease
7. $33\frac{1}{3}$% increase
8. 20% decrease
9. 15% increase
10. 2% increase
11. 30% decrease
12. 10% increase
13. 50% increase
14. 20% decrease
15. $1,480.80
16. $8,391.20

Page 68
1. $75
2. $24
3. $33.75
4. $445.20
5. $87.30
6. $75.60
7. $126
8. $18.80
9. $13.30
10. $31.50
11. $48
12. $24.75
13. I = $960; A = $4,960
14. 6 mo
Mixed Review
1–5. Estimates may vary.
1. about 900
2. about 100
3. about 50%
4. about 25%
5. about 20%

Page 69
1–8. Estimates may vary.
1. about $3.00
2. about $3.75
3. about $0.90
4. about $1.80
5. about $4.50
6. about $4.50
7. about $3.00
8. about $1.50
9. about $10.50
10. about $40
11. I = $3,840; A = $11,840
12. 3 paces
13. about 12,000 square miles

Page 70
1. ⁻27
2. 20
3. ⁻4
4. 4
5. 55
6. 143
7. 0
8. 91

148

Page 70 (cont.)
9. 234
10. ⁻145
11. 81
12. biking west 3 km
13. earning $25
14. falling 5°C
15. <
16. >
17. <
18. =
19. ⁻5, ⁻3, 2, 3
20. ⁻17, ⁻5, ⁻2, 17
21. ⁻10, ⁻7, 2, 4, 5
22. 20, ⁻20
23. 6:00 P.M. to midnight
24. ⁻273

Page 71
1. 7
2. ⁻7
3. ⁻5
4. 5
5. ⁻7
6. ⁻8
7. 3
8. ⁻9
9. 2
10. ⁻8
11. 11
12. 45
13. 20
14. 0
15. 10
16. ⁻8
17. ⁻23
18. 3
19. 0
20. 16
21. 52
22. 16
23. ⁻39
24. 17
25. 117
26. ⁻14
27. ⁻69
28. ⁻148
29. 15
30. 15
31. ⁻38
32. 0
33. ⁻6
34. 1
35. ⁻7 m
36. 1,552 customers
37. ⁻19, ⁻14, ⁻9, ⁻4, 1, 6
38. 16 in.
39. ⁻10 and ⁻13; ⁻10

Page 72
1. 17
2. 8
3. ⁻6
4. ⁻6
5. 22
6. ⁻42
7. 8

Page 72 (cont.)
8. 5
9. 16
10. ⁻11
11. 63
12. ⁻14
13. 8
14. 102
15. ⁻22
16. 0
17. 31
18. ⁻118
19. ⁻28
20. 6
21. 3
22. ⁻28
23. 122
24. 0
25. ⁻9
26. ⁻17
27. 0
28. 30 ft higher
29. 118 m
30. ⁻4, ⁻5
31. $\frac{2}{15}$

Mixed Review
1. >
2. <
3. >
4. >
5. <
6. <
7. >
8. >

Page 73
1. 32
2. ⁻32
3. ⁻78
4. ⁻126
5. ⁻21
6. ⁻34
7. ⁻120
8. ⁻90
9. 54
10. ⁻90
11. 153
12. ⁻54
13. 66
14. ⁻39
15. 50
16. ⁻126
17. ⁻68
18. 120
19. ⁻81
20. ⁻36
21. 24
22. 144
23. ⁻80
24. ⁻220
25. ⁻90
26. 150
27. ⁻120
28. 8
29. 40
30. 78
31. ⁻36

Page 73 (cont.)
32. 72
33. ⁻198
34. $25
35. ⁻8 and 7
36. 410 cans

Page 74
1. ⁻11
2. ⁻3
3. ⁻5
4. 33
5. ⁻12
6. 22
7. ⁻25
8. ⁻30
9. ⁻7
10. 12
11. ⁻14
12. ⁻8
13. ⁻66
14. 4
15. 79
16. ⁻156
17. 100
18. ⁻24
19. 50 days
20. 24 in. shorter
21. N
22. N
23. $200

Page 75
1. Commutative Property
2. Identity Property
3. Associative Property
4. Identity Property
5. Additive Inverse Property
6. Distributive Property
7. ⁻4
8. 238
9. 2
10. 33
11. ⁻10
12. 422
13. 7
14. ⁻160
15. 68 m
16. 22 lines
17. 27 mi

Page 76
1. 5^{-1}
2. 10^{-7}
3. 8^{-3}
4. 10^{-2}
5. 2^{-5}
6. 8^{-2}
7. 3^{-3}
8. 10^{-6}
9. 5^{-2}
10. $\frac{1}{10,000}$; or 0.0001
11. $\frac{1}{10,000,000}$; or 0.0000001
12. $\frac{1}{1,000,000}$; or 0.000001
13. $\frac{1}{32}$; or 0.03125
14. $\frac{1}{3}$; or $0.\overline{3}$

Page 76 (cont.)

15. $\frac{1}{10}$; or 0.1
16. $\frac{1}{81}$
17. $\frac{1}{125}$; or 0.008
18. $\frac{1}{81}$
19. $\frac{1}{100}$; or 0.01
20. $\frac{1}{16}$; or 0.0625
21. $\frac{1}{121}$
22. $\frac{-1}{6}$, or $-0.1\overline{6}$
23. $\frac{-1}{27}$
24. $\frac{1}{25}$; or 0.04
25. $\frac{1}{64}$; or 0.015625
26. $\frac{-1}{12}$; or $-0.08\overline{3}$
27. $\frac{1}{144}$
28. negative exponent
29. positive exponent
30. No; All the numbers are the quotient of 1 and a positive number, thus all the numbers are positive.

Page 77

1. $1 + 9$
2. $4 + {}^-4$
3. $2 - ({}^-3)$
4. ${}^-9 - ({}^-9)$
5. ${}^-10 - 1$
6. ${}^-7 - ({}^-2)$
7. 2^{10}
8. 4^9
9. 8^{11}
10. 14^{-6}
11. 9^{-9}
12. 3^1
13. 7^{-8}
14. 6^{13}
15. $({}^-10)^5$
16. $({}^-5)^{-5}$
17. $({}^-6)^{-1}$
18. 4^1
19. 10^5
20. 12^1
21. 8^2
22. 9^9
23. 11^{-12}
24. 3^1
25. 10^3
26. 2^{-12}
27. $({}^-9)^9$
28. $({}^-7)^{-10}$
29. $(4.2)^{-1}$
30. 7^{25} bacteria

Page 78

1. 1.2×10^4
2. 5.7×10^{10}
3. 4.3×10^{-4}
4. 8.76×10^{-9}
5. 2.4×10^{-3}
6. 1.7×10^{-7}
7. 9×10^{-6}

Page 78 (cont.)

8. 8.045×10^7
9. 6.3×10^9
10. 6×10^{-7}
11. 400,000
12. 5,700
13. 9,000,000
14. 500
15. 33,000,000
16. 0.0009
17. 0.064
18. 2,300
19. 900,000
20. 0.0000005
21. 6.7×10^{-6}
22. 385 million
23. 1.25×10^7; 9.2×10^{-4}

Page 79

1. ${}^-13$ m
2. $9.50
3. ${}^-7°F$
4. $7°F$ per hour
5. 135 gal
6. Brand B
7. Check problem.

Page 80

1. $\frac{5}{10}$
2. $\frac{7}{3}$
3. $\frac{4}{1}$
4. $\frac{26}{10}$
5. $\frac{8}{10}$
6. $\frac{-15}{4}$
7. $\frac{225}{100}$
8. $\frac{9}{5}$
9. >
10. <
11. <
12. <
13. $-2, -1\frac{2}{3}, \frac{1}{4}$
14. $\frac{4}{7}, \frac{3}{4}, 1\frac{2}{3}, 2, 2.3$
15. $-1\frac{1}{3}, -1.3, \frac{2}{5}, \frac{3}{6}, \frac{2}{3}$
16. $1, 1\frac{2}{5}, 1.45, 2\frac{3}{8}, 2.7$
17. 8:00 A.M.
18. descend
19. $10°C$
20. $40°C$
21. ${}^-17.8°C$

Page 81

1. SR
2. SR
3. S
4. N
5. SR
6. 9
7. 196
8. 49
9. 169
10. 256
11. 0.36

Page 81 (cont.)

12. $\frac{16}{25}$
13. $\frac{25}{144}$
14. $\frac{169}{36}$
15. $11, {}^-11$
16. $16, {}^-16$
17. $14, {}^-14$
18. $20, {}^-20$
19. $30, {}^-30$
20. 7
21. ${}^-9$
22. 12
23. ${}^-8$
24. 15
25. 18 s
26. 120 m
27. 11

Page 82

1. 9.4
2. 11.1
3. 4.5
4. ${}^-7.8$
5. 1.73
6. 4.12
7. ${}^-5.83$
8. 9.33
9. 11.14
10. 10.54
11. 0.20
12. ${}^-0.46$
13. 2.2
14. 7
15. 3.3
16. 7.1
17. 5.5
18. No; The graph is not accurate enough.
19. Possible answers: Advantage: quick estimation of square roots. Disadvantage: does not give accurate values.

Page 83

2. Real, Rational, Whole, Integer
3. Real, Rational
4. Real, Irrational
5. Real, Irrational
6. Real, Rational, Integer
7. Real, Rational
8. Real, Rational
9. Real, Rational
10. ${}^-10, {}^-9.1, {}^-\sqrt{13}, (0.39)^2, 3.14159\ldots, 6\frac{1}{3}, 7.21212\ldots, 210, 312$
11. 7; real, rational, whole, integer
12. $3.74\ldots$, real, irrational
13. $0.42\ldots$, real, irrational
14. 0.9; real, rational
15. 7, 63, 28

Page 84

1. $\frac{1}{3}$
2. $\frac{1}{8}$
3. $2\frac{7}{9}$

Page 84 (cont.)

4. $\frac{-3}{5}$
5. $\frac{-1}{4}$
6. $-6\frac{4}{7}$
7. -6.2
8. -0.6
9. -11.33
10. $\frac{13}{12}$, or $1\frac{1}{12}$
11. $\frac{-5}{14}$
12. $1\frac{11}{104}$
13. $\frac{1}{5}$
14. $\frac{5}{22}$
15. $\frac{-7}{18}$
16. 4.2
17. 8.75
18. 5.19
19. 4.79
20. -6.79
21. -30.69
22. $5\frac{1}{4}$ dozen eggs
23. 32.9°C
24. less than the original number

Page 85

1. Randy: Coast Guard; Joe: Army; Paul: Air Force
2. Chuck: shortstop; Mary: pitcher; Tai: catcher; Tyrone: first base
3. 35 years old
4. Yellow brand; $102.76 for 200
5. 6

Page 86

1. $\frac{-1}{18}$
2. $\frac{3}{25}$
3. $\frac{-4}{21}$
4. $\frac{-16}{39}$
5. -1
6. $\frac{-1}{2}$
7. $\frac{5}{16}$
8. $\frac{-35}{72}$
9. -1.08
10. -13.68
11. 1
12. 20
13. -4
14. -17.1
15. -0.624
16. $\frac{-8}{15}$
17. -25
18. -1
19. -1.68
20. 9.3
21. 6.2
22. 3
23. -3.15
24. -0.3
25. 8

Page 86 (cont.)

26. 0.4
27. 2
28. 14.78 inches
29. 27 years
30. Check problem.

Page 87

1. $a = -6$
2. $b = 5$
3. $c = 16$
4. $d = 14.3$
5. $e = 2$
6. $f = -5.5$
7. $g = 0.9$
8. $h = -9$
9. $j = 49$
10. $k = 4.3$
11. $m = -2.99$
12. $n = -9$
13–15. Variables will vary.
13. $x + 1.3 = 3.2$
14. $y - 6.3 = -6.3$
15. $\frac{4}{5}c = 32$; $c = 40$; 40 cars
16. 12.7 inches

Mixed Review

1. 36
2. 15%
3. 80
4. 43.2
5. 2.88
6. 40%

Page 88

1. $a = -2$
2. $b = 2$
3. $c = 29$
4. $f = -0.5$
5. $h = -2$
6. $y = 1$
7. $j = -2$
8. $k = 0.7$
9. $w = -1$
10. $m = -45$
11. $n = 28$
12. $r = -9$
13–15. Key sequences may vary.
13. $6 - 5 = x\ 4 \div 3$
14. $6 + 3 = x\ 3 \div 2$
15. $2.1 - 3 = x\ 7 \div 3$
16. $2x - 3 = 15$; $x = 9$; 9 goals
17. 66 dolls
18. a

Page 89

1–9. See page 156 for number lines.
1. $a < -1$
2. $b > 14$
3. $c < 1.5$
4. $d \geq 10$
5. $e < 5$
6. $f > -7$
7. $t \leq -0.75$
8. $y > -2$
9. $s > -2$

Page 89 (cont.)

10. $2n - 40 < 120$; $n < 80$; less than 80 were sold in April and less than 40 in May.
11. $16\frac{1}{3}$ mi

Mixed Review

1. $\frac{3}{8}$
2. $-3\frac{4}{7}$
3. $\frac{5}{36}$
4. 12
5. -109
6. 10

Page 90

1. 4 hrs 48 min
2. 30 miles
3. $7.29
4. 53 black, 159 white
5. 60.6 miles per hour
6. 25.5 square feet
7. 12

Page 91

1. (6, 3)
2. (3, -2)
3. (-2, 3)
4. (2, 4)
5. (-4, -4)
6. (-6, 2)
7. (5, -7)
8. (-2, -6)
9. (-2, 1)
10. (4, 6)
11. (1, -3)
12. (-3, -2)
13. P
14. N
15. K
16. M
17. Q
18. R
19–26. See page 156.
27. 4 blocks
28. 70%
29. Base I (3, 7); Base II (5, -5); Base III (-3, 0)

Page 92

1. (-4, -4), (1, 1), (3, 3), (-2, -2); yes
2. (-3, 2), (1, -4), (4, 1), (4, -2); no
3. Multiply each hour value by $10.
4. Subtract $5 from each original price.
5.

Growth of Plant				
Years, x	1	2	3	4	5
Height, y	28 in.	32 in.	36 in.	40 in.	44 in.

6. 3 hr
7. Check problem.

Page 93

1–3. Answers may vary.
1. (-2, 3), (-1, 4), (0, 5), (1, 6)
2. (-2, -5), (-1, -4), (0, -3), (1, -2)

151

Page 93 (cont.)
3. (⁻2, ⁻4), (⁻1, ⁻2), (0, 0), (1, 2)
4. no
5. no
6. yes
7. no
8–10. Check table.
8. $y = 2 - x$; (⁻1, 3), ($\frac{-1}{2}$, 2$\frac{1}{2}$), (0, 2), ($\frac{1}{2}$, 1$\frac{1}{2}$), (1, 1)
9. $y = 10 - 4x$; (⁻1, 14), ($\frac{-1}{2}$, 12), (0, 10), ($\frac{1}{2}$, 8), (1, 6)
10. $y = 10 - x$; (⁻1, 11), ($\frac{-1}{2}$, 10$\frac{1}{2}$), (0, 10), ($\frac{1}{2}$, 9$\frac{1}{2}$), (1, 9)
11. $y = x + 3$
12. 1.5 hr listening; 3 hr reading
13. 64 km

Page 94
1. (2, 4)
2. (⁻6, ⁻4)
3. $x = 0$
4. One solution is (4, 6).
5–8. Check graphs. Possible ordered pairs are given.
5. (⁻1, ⁻3), (0, ⁻2), (2, 0)
6. (⁻2, ⁻3), (0, 1), (2, 5)
7. (⁻5, 0), (0, 5), (2, 7)
8. (⁻2, ⁻6), (0, 0), (1, 3)
9. $y = 2x$; Check graph.
10. 8 hr
11. an infinite number

Page 95
1. about 15 sec
2. about $\frac{4}{5}$, or 0.8 mi
3. about 50 sec
4. 21.25 m
5. $101.50
Mixed Review
1. $a = 24$
2. $x = 100$
3. $z = 2$
4. $y = 31$
5. 7
6. ⁻1
7. 3

Page 96
1. $\frac{1}{1}$, or 1
2. $\frac{4}{3}$
3. $\frac{1}{2}$
4. $\frac{3}{2}$
5. $\frac{-1}{2}$
6. $\frac{-3}{1}$, or ⁻3
7. 0
8. $\frac{3}{1}$, or 3
9. $\frac{2}{7}$
10. negative
11. negative

Page 96 (cont.)
12. positive
13. negative
14. positive
15. positive
16. $\frac{14}{51}$

Page 97
1–3. See page 156.
1. (1, ⁻1)
2. (1, 5)
3. (⁻1, ⁻4)
4. $x + y = 15$; $y = x + 3$; Mark: 9 hr; John: 6 hr
5. $x + y = 18$; $y = 2x$; Jogging: 12 hr; Sit-ups: 6 hr
Mixed Review
1. $\frac{10}{2}$, or 5
2. $\frac{13}{4}$, or 3$\frac{1}{4}$
3. $\frac{11}{10}$, or 1$\frac{1}{10}$
4. $\frac{2}{5}$
5. $\frac{-4}{3}$, or ⁻1$\frac{1}{3}$
6. $\frac{17}{21}$
7. $\frac{2}{9}$
8. $\frac{35}{3}$, or 11$\frac{2}{3}$
9. $\frac{110}{13}$, or 8$\frac{6}{13}$
10. $\frac{16}{15}$, or 1$\frac{1}{15}$
11. $\frac{12}{77}$
12. $\frac{8}{27}$

Page 98
1–3. See page 156.
4. Possible answer: (⁻2, 6)
5. no
6. Possible answer: (1, 6)
7. 5 boxes
8. (0, 5), (3, 3), (6, 1)
9. 7,753

Page 99
1. (3, 2)
2. (⁻1, 8)
3. (3, 4)
4. (3, ⁻6)
5. (5, ⁻2)
6. (2, 0)
7. (⁻4, ⁻5)
8. (⁻4, 1)
9. (3, 5)
10. (2, ⁻8)
11–13. See page 156.
14. A′(5, ⁻7), B′(5, ⁻2), C′(1, ⁻4), D′(1, ⁻6)
15. 10:30 A.M.
16. Check drawing.

Page 100
1. 2 student tickets; 1 adult ticket
2. 4 records; 3 tapes
3. 4 local; 2 city
4. 3 pens; 3 pencils
5. 4,096 newspapers

Page 100 (cont.)
6. 16 hot dogs, 1 soda; 13 hot dogs, 5 sodas; 10 hot dogs, 9 sodas; 7 hot dogs, 13 sodas; 4 hot dogs, 17 sodas; 1 hot dog, 21 sodas
7. 68 people

Page 101
1. 75.71; 75; 75, 80
2. 5.76; 5.12; no mode
3. 5 lbs; 5 lbs; no mode
4. 29; 25; 25
5. 75, 80
6. 75
7. false
8. false
9. 3; 3; 3
10. 21 hours
11. Check problem.

Page 102
1. See page 156.
2. 19
3. 3 students
4. women
5. 18 people
6. Check graph.

Page 103
1. a
2. See page 156.
3. 4.9 inches
4. Morgantown
5. Check answer.

Page 104
1. sufficient; yes
2. insufficient
3. sufficient; 40°F
4. sufficient; 13°F
5. 60
6. $12
Mixed Review
1. $5,200
2. $4,625
3. no mode

Page 105
1. See page 156.
2. Norfolk
3. Norfolk
4. Albany
5. 4.4 inches
6. Chicago
7. 848 miles
8. Check answer.

Page 106
1. 14 games
2. 50%
3. 35.7%
4. 14.3%
5. 180°
6. 129°
7. 51°

Page 106 (cont.)

8. **Shywood Eagles Record**

50% Wins
35.7% Losses
14.3% Ties

9. Ties and Losses together equal 50% of the games.
10. 67%
11. 270°

Page 107

1–3. See page 156 for line graph.
1. Increasing over time
2. $40 million
3. $280 million
4. $105 million
5. $205 million
6. $83.61 million
7. Possible answer: Avg. income to estimate tax revenue.

Page 108

1. 6
2. 2
3. 4
4. 9
5. 18
6. 6
7. 3
8. 300
9. $1.20
10. Check answer.

Page 109

1. 24
2. 6,720
3. 19,958,400
4. 18
5. 26
6. $\frac{5!}{2!}$
7. 5!
8. $\frac{7!}{2!}$
9. $\frac{20!}{17!}$
10. 4!
11. 380
12. 2,730
13. 5,040
14. 1,680
15. 332,640
16. 12; 120; 360; 15,120
17. 72 ways
18. 3 students
19. 42 ways

Page 110

1. $\frac{1}{8}$
2. $\frac{7}{8}$
3. $\frac{1}{4}$
4. $\frac{3}{8}$

Page 110 (cont.)

5. $\frac{1}{8}$
6. $\frac{1}{2}$
7. $\frac{1}{6}$
8. $\frac{1}{3}$
9. $\frac{5}{6}$
10. $\frac{1}{2}$
11. $\frac{1}{2}$
12. 0
13. hhh, hht, hth, thh, tth, htt, tht, ttt
14. $\frac{1}{2}$
15. $\frac{1}{4}$

Mixed Review

1. $\frac{4}{5}$
2. $\frac{8}{5}$ or $1\frac{3}{5}$
3. $\frac{7}{10}$
4. $\frac{2}{9}$
5. $\frac{4}{3}$
6. 35
7. 18

Page 111

1. Row 2: 2; Row 3: 3, 3; Row 4: 4, 6, 4
2. $\frac{1}{16}$
3. $\frac{1}{16}$
4. $\frac{4}{16}$ or $\frac{1}{4}$
5. $\frac{1}{32}$
6. $\frac{5}{32}$
7. $\frac{5}{32}$
8. 1, 5, 10, 10, 5, 1,
9. 1, 6, 15, 20, 15, 6, 1
10. 1, 2, 4, 8, 16, 32
11. 8
12. The first and last numbers are 1. Each number in between is the sum of the two above it.

Page 112

1. 210 combinations
2. 66 ways
3. 84 ways
4. 210 ways
5. 10! or 3,628,800
6. $2,450
7. 57.14 mph
8. $146\frac{2}{3}$ mi

Mixed Review

1. $x = 27$
2. $x = 10$
3. $x = 15.2$
4. b

Page 113

1. 20 spins
2. 9 spins
3. 4 times

Page 113 (cont.)

4. $\frac{1}{10}$
5. 5 times; 4 times fewer
6. $120
7. Check answer.

Page 114

1. $\frac{3}{5}$, or 0.6
2. $\frac{2}{5}$, or 0.4
3. 45 times
4. 10 times
5. $\frac{7}{10}$, or 0.7
6. 6
7. $\frac{1}{4}$, or 0.25
8. $\frac{13}{40}$, or 0.325
9. 103
10. 38.33%

Page 115

1. $\frac{1}{24}$
2. $\frac{1}{4}$
3. $\frac{1}{8}$
4. $\frac{5}{24}$
5. 0
6. $\frac{1}{6}$
7. $\frac{1}{32}$
8. $\frac{1}{16}$
9. $\frac{3}{8}$
10. $\frac{7}{16}$
11. $\frac{1}{32}$
12. $\frac{1}{16}$
13. $\frac{1}{2}$
14. 35 questions

Mixed Review

1. $\frac{1}{8}$
2. $\frac{2}{15}$
3. $\frac{17}{6}$
4. mean: 80; median: 79; mode: 73

Page 116

1. $\frac{1}{15}$
2. $\frac{1}{9}$
3. $\frac{2}{9}$
4. $\frac{1}{12}$
5. $\frac{1}{60}$
6. $\frac{1}{120}$
7. $\frac{1}{24}$
8. $\frac{1}{14}$
9. $\frac{1}{6}$
10. $\frac{1}{26}$
11. $\frac{1}{13}$
12. $\frac{1}{13}$

Page 116 (cont.)

13. $\frac{1}{13} \times \frac{1}{17} = \frac{1}{221}$

14. Check question.

Page 117

1.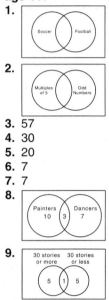

2.

3. 57
4. 30
5. 20
6. 7
7. 7
8.

9.

Page 118

1. 1 m
2. $\frac{1}{4}$ ft
3. $\frac{1}{8}$ in.
4. 0.1 km
5. 0.5 mm
6. $\frac{1}{2}$ yd
7. 0.05 m
8. 0.005 km
9. $\frac{1}{8}$ ft
10. $\frac{1}{6}$ mi
11. 0.0005 m
12. $\frac{1}{32}$ ft
13. $49\frac{1}{2}$ mi; $50\frac{1}{2}$ mi
14. 59.5 mm; 60.5 mm
15. 34.45 km; 34.55 km
16. $11\frac{1}{4}$ yd; $11\frac{3}{4}$ yd
17. $\frac{1}{2}$ ft
18. $11\frac{1}{2}$ ft; $12\frac{1}{2}$ ft
19. Check question.

Page 119

1. 1
2. 3
3. 2
4. 30 m
5. 10.2 m
6. 10.63 m
7. 5 m²
8. 8 m²
9. 3.9 m²
10. 4
11. 3

Page 119 (cont.)
Mixed Review

1. $\frac{1}{4}$
2. 7
3. $\frac{5}{3}$
4. $\frac{8}{6}$
5. 4.6
6. 2.00
7. 4.684

Page 120

1. 4
2. 144
3. 6
4. 16
5. $47\frac{1}{2}$ cups
6. $220
7. 2,700 miles
8. 99 pounds
9. Check drawing.

Page 121

1. 17 cm
2. 28 m
3. 30 ft
4. 40 in.
5. 6 m
6. 18 ft
7. 3.4 cm
8. 12 in.
9. no
10. 110 ft
11. Check question.

Page 122

1. 25.47 cm
2. 0.19 cm
3. 1.51 m
4. 2.89 km
5. 44 in.
6. 132 yd
7. 176 ft
8. 220 ft
9. 42 ft
10. 0.5 m
11. 100 in.
12. perimeter of the square
13. 9.42 m
14. 31.4 ft

Mixed Review

1. 20 cm
2. 80 m
3. 16 km
4. 24 cm
5. 28 yd
6. 21
7. ⁻54
8. 56

Page 123

1. 24 m²
2. 49 ft²
3. 40 in.²

Page 123 (cont.)

4. 18 in.²
5. 96 m²
6. 62.98 m²
7. 40 m²
8. 66 m²
9. 140 in.²
10. Yes, if either the length or width respectively do not exceed the length and width of the hall.
11. Check answer.

Page 124

1. 12 cm²
2. 25 ft²
3. 18 cm²
4. 54 m²
5. 45 m²
6. 172 m²
7. 130 m²
8. 6 ft²
9. Check design.

Page 125

1. 50.24 cm²
2. 314 m²
3. 191.04 m²
4. 241.78 cm²
5. 150.72 cm²
6. 34.24 in.²
7. 78.5 m²
8. 37.68 in.

Mixed Review

1. 80
2. 22
3. 5
4. 21
5. 0.15
6. 0.16
7. 0.06
8. 0.5

Page 126

1. 8 rolls
2. 90 rolls
3. $120
4. 11 rolls
5. $1,256
6. 24 bricks
7. Check answer.

Page 127

1. pyramid; rectangular pyramid
2. pyramid; triangular pyramid
3. pyramid; pentagonal pyramid
4. prism; hexagonal prism
5. 2 square bases; other faces parallelograms
6. 2 triangular bases; other faces parallelograms
7. 2 rectangular bases; other faces parallelograms
8. 40 inches or 3 feet 4 inches
9. rectangular prism; television will not fit in pyramid.
10. c

Page 128
1. sphere
2. cylinder
3. cone
4. sphere
5. cone
6. cylindrical; easy to hold
7. spherical; can roll
8. 7.85 inches
9. 3.34 inches
10. 4.00×10^7 m
11. 2.40×10^9 m
12. 9.42×10^{11} m

Page 129
1.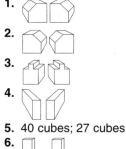
2.
3.
4.
5. 40 cubes; 27 cubes
6.
7. Check drawing.

Page 130
1. 69 cm²
2. 77.98 m²
3. 144 m²
4. 233.63 cm²
5. 32.64 in.²
6. 142.8 m²
7. 67.5 m²
8. 4 gallons of paint
9. 946,015 ft

Page 131
1. $\pi r l$
2. 2, 2, h
3. 75.36 cm²
4. 65.9 cm²
5. 314 cm²
6. 125.6 cm²
7. 35.3 cm²
8. 235.5 cm²
9. 207.2 cm²
10. 205.0 cm²
11. 21.1 cm²
12. 62.8 cm²
13. 62.1 cm²
14. 33.5 cm²
15. 115.4 cm²
16. 3.141593

Page 132
1. 1.75 ft³
2. 3 m³
3. 6.6 cm³
4. 10 m³
5. 880 cm³
6. 6 ft³

Page 132 (cont.)
7. 4.5 cm³
8. 9 m³
9. 22.8 m³
10. 10 cm x 10 cm x 10 cm
11. 6.25 ft
12. Find $\frac{2}{3}$ the volume of a cube with the same side.

Page 133
1. 65 m³
2. 339 ft³
3. 49 in.³
4. 13 in.³
5. 4,974 ft³
6. 12 m³
7. 37.7 m³
8. 8 m
Mixed Review
1. 61.4 cm²
2. 22.9 cm²

Page 134
1. 6.7
2. 3.2
3. 16.8 mL; 16.8 g
4. 40 L; 40 kg
5. 4.91 L; 4.91 kg
6. 19.44 mL; 19.44 g
7. 5.28 L; 5.28 kg
8. 33.5 L; 33.5 kg
9. 785 g
10. 704.8 g
11. 100 L

Page 135
1. 39 tennis balls
2. 381.51 g
3. 102.96 in.³
4. 27 oranges
5. 1 hour
6. $537.50
7. $2.84
8. about 24 min 31 sec
9. 5 trips

Page 136
1. hypotenuse, $\overline{BC}$; legs, $\overline{AC}$, $\overline{AB}$
2. hypotenuse, $\overline{DE}$; legs, $\overline{DF}$, $\overline{EF}$
3. hypotenuse, $\overline{GI}$; legs, $\overline{HI}$, $\overline{HG}$
4. hypotenuse, $\overline{BC}$; legs, $\overline{AB}$, $\overline{AC}$
5. hypotenuse, $\overline{DF}$; legs, $\overline{DE}$, $\overline{EF}$
6. hypotenuse, $\overline{GI}$; legs, $\overline{HI}$, $\overline{GH}$
7. no
8. yes
9. yes
10. no
11. yes
12. no
Mixed Review
1. 720
2. 362,880
3. 479,001,600
4. 1,680
5. 30,240

Page 136 (cont.)
6. $\frac{4!}{(4-2)!}$
7. $\frac{7!}{(7-3)!}$
8. $\frac{10!}{(10-4)!}$
9. $\frac{10!}{(10-3)!}$
10. $\frac{12!}{(12-5)!}$

Page 137
1. $a = 5$ m
2. $b = 5.7$ mm
3. $a = 5.4$ m
4. $c = 2.2$ mm
5. 16.2 m
6. 62.6 ft
7. 33.5 m
8. 46.6 ft
9. 10 yrs old
10. 35 ft; Check problem.

Page 138
1. $5\sqrt{2}$
2. $7\sqrt{2}$
3. $\frac{(3\sqrt{2})}{2}$
4. $6\sqrt{2}$
5. 3
6. $2\sqrt{3}$
7. $5\sqrt{3}$
8. 18
9. about 14.2 ft
10. $45\sqrt{2}$ ft
Mixed Review
1. ⁻9
2. ⁻14
3. ⁻12
4. 36
5. ⁻42
6. 5
7. 16
8. 0

Page 139
1. $15
2. Choice 3
3. $14
4. Check answer.
5. 9.1 mi
6. from 5 to 7 gifts
7. Check problem.

Page 140
1. yes
2. yes
3. yes
4. $x = 20$ mm
5. $x = 1.5$ m
6. yes
7. 5
8. Possible answer: The height of the ruler is proportional to the height of the flag pole. You can use that ratio to find the distance to the flag pole.

Core Skills: Math, Grade 8, Graphics

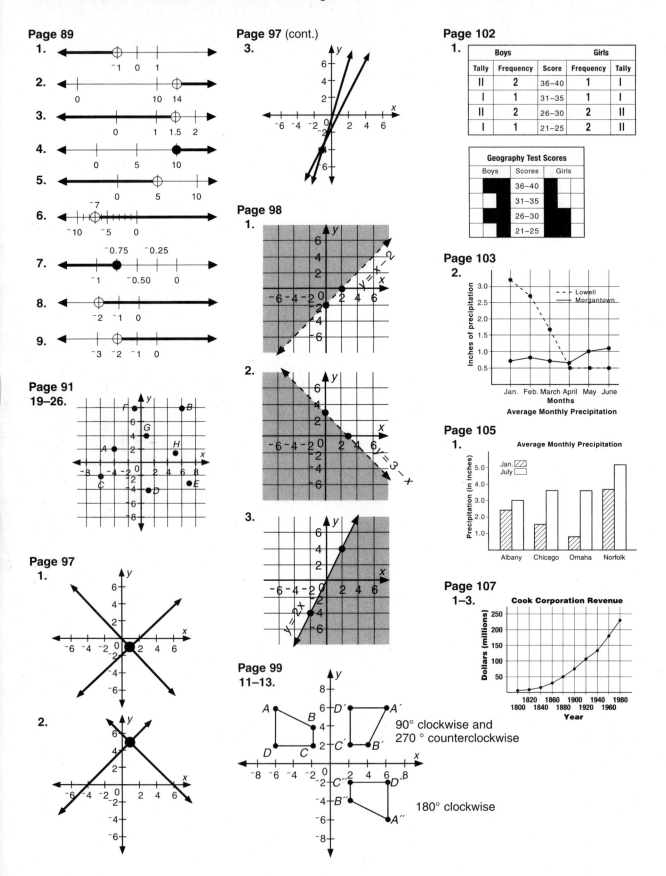

Page 89

1.
2.
3.
4.
5.
6.
7.
8.
9.

Page 91
19–26.

Page 97
1.
2.

Page 97 (cont.)
3.

Page 98
1.
2.
3.

Page 99
11–13.

90° clockwise and 270° counterclockwise

180° clockwise

Page 102

1.

Boys			Girls	
Tally	Frequency	Score	Frequency	Tally
II	2	36–40	1	I
I	1	31–35	1	I
II	2	26–30	2	II
I	1	21–25	2	II

Geography Test Scores		
Boys	Scores	Girls
	36–40	
	31–35	
	26–30	
	21–25	

Page 103
2.

Average Monthly Precipitation

Page 105
1.

Average Monthly Precipitation

Page 107
1–3.

Cook Corporation Revenue

156